REVOLUTION

Volume 30

STUDIES IN REVOLUTION

STUDIES IN REVOLUTION

EDWARD HALLETT CARR

LONDON AND NEW YORK

First published in 1950 by Macmillan & Co
Reprinted with corrections in 1962 by Frank Cass & Co Ltd

This edition first published in 2022
by Routledge
4 Park Square, Milton Park, Abingdon, Oxon OX14 4RN

and by Routledge
605 Third Avenue, New York, NY 10158

Routledge is an imprint of the Taylor & Francis Group, an informa business

© 1962 Frank Cass & Co Ltd

All rights reserved. No part of this book may be reprinted or reproduced or utilised in any form or by any electronic, mechanical, or other means, now known or hereafter invented, including photocopying and recording, or in any information storage or retrieval system, without permission in writing from the publishers.

Trademark notice: Product or corporate names may be trademarks or registered trademarks, and are used only for identification and explanation without intent to infringe.

British Library Cataloguing in Publication Data
A catalogue record for this book is available from the British Library

ISBN: 978-1-032-12623-4 (Set)
ISBN: 978-1-003-26095-0 (Set) (ebk)
ISBN: 978-1-032-17133-3 (Volume 30) (hbk)
ISBN: 978-1-032-17134-0 (Volume 30) (pbk)
ISBN: 978-1-003-25193-4 (Volume 30) (ebk)

DOI: 10.4324/9781003251934

Publisher's Note
The publisher has gone to great lengths to ensure the quality of this reprint but points out that some imperfections in the original copies may be apparent.

Disclaimer
The publisher has made every effort to trace copyright holders and would welcome correspondence from those they have been unable to trace.

STUDIES IN REVOLUTION

BY
EDWARD HALLETT CARR

FRANK CASS & CO LTD
1962

First Published by
Macmillan & Co 1950

Reprinted with corrections
by Frank Cass & Co Ltd
10 Woburn Walk London WC2
in 1962

Made and printed in Great Britain by
Charles Birchall and Sons Ltd Liverpool and London

CONTENTS

	PAGE
1. SAINT-SIMON: THE PRECURSOR (1949)	1
2. THE *COMMUNIST MANIFESTO* (1947)	15
3. PROUDHON: ROBINSON CRUSOE OF SOCIALISM (1947)	38
4. HERZEN: AN INTELLECTUAL REVOLUTIONARY (1947)	56
5. LASSALLE MEETS BISMARCK (1946)	72
6. SOME NINETEENTH-CENTURY RUSSIAN THINKERS (1947)	88
7. PLEKHANOV: FATHER OF RUSSIAN MARXISM (1948)	105
8. THE CRADLE OF BOLSHEVISM (1948)	120
9. LENIN: THE MASTER BUILDER (1947)	134
10. SOREL: PHILOSOPHER OF SYNDICALISM (1947)	152
11. MR. GALLACHER AND THE CPGB (1949)	166
12. THE REVOLUTION THAT FAILED (1949)	181
13. STALIN: (1) THE ROAD TO POWER (1946)	200
14. STALIN: (2) THE DIALECTICS OF STALINISM (1949)	211

PREFACE

THE articles out of which this book has been made appeared in the *Literary Supplement* of *The Times* and I am indebted to the Editor of the *Supplement* for kind permission to republish them: I have also incorporated in " The Revolution that Failed " some passages from a talk given in the Third Programme of the British Broadcasting Corporation. A few topical references have been adjusted, a few cases of overlapping removed, and a few corrections made to meet criticisms, public or private. Otherwise the articles appear substantially unchanged; the year of original publication is appended to each in the list of contents. Of the two articles on Stalin with which the volume ends, the first was the earliest item in the collection to be written, the second the last.

E. H. CARR

1

SAINT-SIMON: THE PRECURSOR

HENRI DE SAINT-SIMON was an intellectual eccentric. He was a member of an aristocratic family who abandoned his title of *Comte* with a dramatic gesture in the French Revolution and spent most of his life in penury; a rationalist and a moralist; a man of letters who never succeeded in writing or completing any coherent exposition of his ideas; and, after his death, the eponymous father of a sect devoted to the propagation of his teaching, which enjoyed a European reputation. Saint-Simon lacked most of the traditional attributes of the great man. It is never easy to distinguish between what he himself thought and the much more coherent body of doctrine, some of it astonishingly penetrating, some not less astonishingly silly, which the sect built up round his name. It is certain that posterity has read back into some of his aphorisms a greater clarity and a greater significance than he himself gave to them. But the study of Saint-Simon often seems to suggest that the great French Revolution, not content with the ideas which inspired its leaders and which it spread over the contemporary world, also projected into the future

Studies in Revolution

a fresh ferment of ideas which, working beneath the surface, were to be the main agents of the social and political revolutions of one hundred years to come.

Of these ideas Saint-Simon provided the first precipitation on the printed page. No one who writes about him can avoid applying to him the word " precursor ". He was the precursor of socialism, the precursor of the technocrats, the precursor of totalitarianism — all these labels fit, not perfectly, but, considering the distance of time and the originality of the conceptions as first formulated, with amazing appositeness. Saint-Simon died at the age of sixty-five in 1825, on the eve of a period of unprecedented material progress and sweeping social and political change; and his writings again and again gave an uncanny impression of one who has had a hurried preview of the next hundred years of history and, excited, confused and only half under-standing, tried to set down disjointed fragments of what he had seen. He is the type of the great man as the reflector, rather than the maker, of history.

The approach of Saint-Simon to the phenomenon of man in society already has the modern stamp. In 1783, at the age of twenty-three, he had recorded his life's ambition: "Faire un travail scientifique utile à l'humanité". Saint-Simon marks the transition from the deductive rationalism of the eighteenth to the inductive rationalism of the nineteenth century—from metaphysics to science. He inaugurates the cult of science and of the scientific method. He rejects equally the " divine order " of the theo-

Saint-Simon: The Precursor

logians and the "natural order" of Adam Smith and the physiocrats. In his first published writing, *Lettres d'un habitant de Genève*, he enunciated the principle that "social relations must be considered as physiological phenomena". Or again: "The question of social organization must be treated absolutely in the same way as any other scientific question". The term "sociology" was apparently the invention of Saint-Simon's most famous pupil, once his secretary, Auguste Comte. But the idea came from the master himself and was the essence of his philosophy.

Another of Saint-Simon's pupils, Augustin Thierry, was to become a famous historian; and there is in Saint-Simon not only an embryonic sociology, but an embryonic theory of history which looks forward to a whole school from Buckle to Spengler. History is a study of the scientific laws governing human development, which is divided into "époques organiques" and into "époques critiques"; and the continuity of past, present and future is clearly established. "History is social physics." No doubt later nineteenth-century and twentieth-century theories of history owe more to Hegel than to Saint-Simon. But they owe most of all to Karl Marx, who combined the metaphysical historicism of Hegel with Saint-Simon's sociological utilitarianism.

But perhaps Saint-Simon's most original insight — original enough at a moment when the French Revolution had consecrated the emancipation and enthronement of the individual after a struggle of

Studies in Revolution

three centuries — was his vision of the coming resubordination of the individual to society. Saint-Simon, though no partisan of revolution in principle (he once said flatly that dictatorship was preferable to revolution), never abated his enthusiasm for the revolution which had overthrown the *ancien régime.* " La féodalité " was always the enemy; incidentally, it may well be due, directly or indirectly, to Saint-Simon that " feudalism " became Marx's chosen label for the pre-bourgeois order of society. Nearly all Saint-Simon's contemporaries, and most western European thinkers for at least two generations to come, took it for granted that liberalism was the natural antithesis, and therefore the predestined successor, of " feudalism ". Saint-Simon saw no reason for the assumption. He was not a reactionary, nor even a conservative; but he was not a liberal either. He was something different — and new.

It was clear to Saint-Simon that, after Descartes and Kant, after Rousseau and the Declaration of the Rights of Man, the cult of individual liberty, of the individual as an end in himself, could go no farther. There are some astonishingly modern echoes in a collection of essays under the title *L'Industrie*, dating from 1816 :

The Declaration of the Rights of Man which has been regarded as the solution of the problem of social liberty was in reality only the statement of the problem.

A passage of *Du système industriel*, in which Saint-Simon a few years later sought to establish the new historical perspective, is worth quoting in full :

Saint-Simon: The Precursor

The maintenance of liberty was bound to be an object of primary attention so long as the feudal and theological system still had some power, because then liberty was exposed to serious and continuous attacks. But to-day one can no longer have the same anxiety in establishing the industrial and scientific system, since this system must necessarily, and without any direct concern in the matter, bring with it the highest degree of liberty in the temporal and in the social sphere.

Or again, and more emphatically:

The vague and metaphysical idea of liberty in circulation to-day, if it continues to be taken as the basis of political doctrines, would tend pre-eminently to hamper the action of the mass on the individual. From this point of view it would be contrary to the development of civilization and to the organization of an ordered system which demands that the parties should be firmly bound to the whole and dependent on it.

The individual, as Saint-Simon puts it elsewhere, depends on " the mass ", and it is the relations of each individual with this " progressively active, expanding and overwhelming mass " which have to be " studied and organized ". Even the word " liberty ", in the first two passages quoted above, has the question-begging adjective " social " quietly appended to it. The proper study of mankind is no longer man, but the masses.

In short, Saint-Simon stood at the point of transition from " feudal " to industrial civilization. He perceived the nature of the transition more clearly than his contemporaries, and read more of its implications. How far he himself foresaw the

Studies in Revolution

practical application of science to industry cannot be ascertained. It was his disciples who hailed the building of railways with an almost religious fervour as the symbol and instrument of social progress (one recalls Lenin's definition of socialism as " the Soviets plus electrification "), and other disciples who in the 1840s founded the Société d'Études du Canal de Suez. But Saint-Simon insisted — it became more and more the *leitmotiv* of everything he wrote — that industrial production was henceforth the main function of society. " Industry ", " production ", " organization " — these were the key words in the Saint-Simonist vocabulary.

Logically enough, therefore, Saint-Simon appears as one of the founders of the nineteenth-century cult of work. The beginnings of it are in Rousseau and Babeuf; but it was Saint-Simon who placed it in the very centre of his system. The conception .of leisure and contemplation as the highest state of mankind died with the last vestiges of the medieval order. " All men will work," wrote Saint-Simon in the *Lettres d'un habitant de Genève*, where so many of his ideas appear in their primary and simplest form; " the obligation is imposed on every man to give constantly to his personal powers a direction useful to society ". Indeed, in a later " Declaration of Principles ", he defines society " as the sum total and union of men engaged in useful work ". Work is no longer a necessity but a virtue. The new principle of morality is " man must work "; and " the happiest nation is the nation in which there are the fewest unemployed ". Saint-Simon provided

Saint-Simon: The Precursor

the moral foundation for the labour theory of value which was being worked out at the same period in England by Ricardo. He also looked forward to the prominence given one hundred years later in the new Soviet gospel to the precept: "He that does not work neither shall he eat".

The generation which followed Saint-Simon was fruitful in the creation of Utopias; and his views on the organization of society and the State, though there is no systematic exposition of them, were among the most popular of his speculations. It need hardly be said that the liberal conception of politics and economics, introduced into France by Adam Smith's disciple J. B. Say, was anathema to Saint-Simon, for whom "politics is the science of production". But the identification is achieved by the subordination of politics to economics, not of economics to politics. This is logical; for since "society rests wholly on industry", which is "the sole source of all riches and all prosperity", it follows that "the state of things most favourable to industry is for that very reason most favourable to society". Government in the old sense is a necessary evil. Its sole purpose is to put and keep men at work; for, unhappily, there are "*fainéants*, that is to say, thieves". But this is a minor and subsidiary function. The supreme authority will be an "economic parliament" (a notion which still had its attractions more than a century later), divided into three chambers concerned respectively with invention, examination and execution.

But Saint-Simon's city of the future presents

Studies in Revolution

other features still more curious. The division of functions is precise. The artists will appeal to the imagination of the worker and excite the appropriate passions. The men of learning " will establish the laws of health of the body social ". (Incidentally these provisions show that the marshalling of art and science in the service of the State is neither new nor peculiar to any one part of Europe.) The " industrials " (in which term Saint-Simon includes producers of all kinds and even traders) will legislate and issue administrative orders. Finally the executive — it is an unexpected climax — will be composed of bankers. It was the age of the great private banks; and the power of credit in the affairs of government and of business was just becoming a current topic. For Saint-Simon, as for Lenin nearly a century later, the banks were the hidden hand that made the wheels of production go round. It was as logical for Saint-Simon to give them a central place in his administrative scheme as for Lenin to treat the nationalization of the banks as the key measure necessary to destroy the economic stranglehold of the bourgeoisie. But what is interesting is to find an embryonic philosophy of planning built up by Saint-Simon round this central executive function of the banks:

The present anarchy of production, which corresponds to the fact that economic relations are being developed without uniform regulation, must give way to the organization of production. Production will not be directed by isolated *entrepreneurs* independent of each other and ignorant of the needs of the people; this task

Saint-Simon: *The Precursor*

will be entrusted to a specific social institution. A central committee of administration, being able to review a broad field of social economy from a higher point of vantage, will regulate it in a manner useful to the whole society, will transfer the means of production into hands appropriate for this purpose, and will be specially concerned to maintain a constant harmony between production and demand. There are institutions which include among their functions a certain degree of organization of economic work: the banks.

Lenin, who quotes this passage at second-hand and is, perhaps, a little jealous for Marx's priority, calls it " a guess of genius, but still only a guess ".

More directly fruitful than these visions of a distant future was the conception, running through Saint-Simon's writing about the State, of a distinction between " government " and " administration ". It recurs in many shapes. Formerly there were spiritual and temporal " powers "; to-day these have given place to scientific and industrial " capacities ". Power, which is an absolute of government, is an oppressive force exercised by men over men; and " the action of man on man is in itself always harmful to the species ". On the other hand, " the only useful action exercised by man is the action of man on things ". This is administration; and " an enlightened society needs only to be administered ". Society is " destined to pass from the governmental or military regime to the administrative or industrial regime after having made sufficient progress in positive sciences and in industry". Saint-Simon does not, like Engels, say that

Studies in Revolution

the State will die away. Even Engels's phrase that " the government of men will be replaced by the administration of things " has not been traced textually to the works of Saint-Simon and his disciples. But the idea is borrowed direct from him. The influence of Saint-Simon on Proudhon and on the development of French syndicalist thought with its contempt for the politics of government is not less obvious.

How far should Saint-Simon be called, not merely a precursor of socialism, but himself a " Socialist " ? The word had apparently not been coined in his lifetime. It cannot be traced back farther than 1827, when it appeared in England in an Owenite publication. Its first recorded use in French is in an article of 1832 in *Le Globe*, a newspaper edited by Saint-Simon's disciples after his death. " Nous ne voulons pas sacrifier ", remarks the article, " la *personnalité* au *socialisme*, pas plus que ce dernier à la personnalité." In this sense of placing the stress on society rather than on the individual, Saint-Simon was a Socialist. But in the more political modern sense many doubts arise. The only occasion when Saint-Simon placed a label on his own political opinions was when he said that he belonged neither to the Conservative Party nor to the Liberal Party but to the *parti industriel*; and while it may be misleading to translate *industriel* by " industrial ", it can hardly be made to mean " Socialist " or even " Labour ". His legislature of *industriels* and executive of bankers came nearer to a benevolent despotism of technocrats or to the managerial society of later speculations.

Saint-Simon: *The Precursor*

On the other hand, Saint-Simon was constantly preoccupied with the well-being of those whom he called, in a much-quoted phrase, " la classe la plus nombreuse et la plus pauvre ". He stood in principle for equality of distribution ("luxury will become useful and moral when the whole nation enjoys it "), though he did not make this square with his desire to adjust rewards to capacities. He believed that " the existence of society depends on the conservation of the right of property ". But he added that every society must decide for itself what things could become objects of private property and on what conditions they might be held; for " the individual right of property can be based only on the common and general utility of the exercise of this right — a utility which may vary with the period ". Not only is the priority of the claims of society over those of the individual once more unequivocally asserted, but the idea of historical relativism is introduced to bar any absolute right. Rejection of the feudal conception of property as the absolute right on which society rests is fundamental to Saint-Simon's thought. The society of the future will be not a society of proprietors but a society of producers.

After Saint-Simon's death his disciples systematized his vague and inchoate pronouncements on this question as on others; and current opinion moved more decisively along lines which he had dimly adumbrated. *Le Globe* carried for some time at the head of each number a set of aphorisms which were supposed to sum up the essentials of the master's teaching:

Studies in Revolution

All social institutions should have as their aim the moral, intellectual and physical improvement of the most numerous and poorest class.

All privileges of birth are abolished without exception.

From each according to his capacity, to each capacity according to its works.

The *Communist Manifesto* sets Saint-Simon side by side with Fourier and Owen as " critical-Utopian Socialists ", who attacked existing society on valid grounds but prescribed Utopian remedies. More specifically, they are accused of failing to appreciate the role of the proletariat in the class struggle or to countenance violent methods of changing the established order. Yet it is fair to recall Engels's handsome tribute — though Saint-Simon would not have liked to be excluded from the " scientific " thinkers — nearly thirty years later :

German theoretical Socialism will never forget that it stands on the shoulders of Saint-Simon, Fourier and Owen — three thinkers who, however fantastic and Utopian their teachings, belong to the great minds of all times and by the intuition of genius anticipated an incalculable number of the truths which we now demonstrate scientifically.

It was at the very end of his life, and after the failure of an attempt at suicide, that Saint-Simon wrote a book under the title *Le Nouveau Christianisme*, which was the first of several nineteenth-century attempts to create a secular religion on a basis of Christian ethics. At an early stage in his career, while professing belief in God, he had declared that

Saint-Simon: The Precursor

" the idea of God cannot be employed in the physical sciences " (in which the social sciences were for Saint-Simon included), adding, however, a little enigmatically that " it is the best method yet found to motivate high legislative decisions ". This pragmatic basis was evidently not lacking in *Le Nouveau Christianisme*, though it purported to be the expression of certain moral absolutes, including the brotherhood of man and the universal obligation to work. The " Catholic system ", Saint-Simon had discovered, was " in contradiction with the system of the sciences and of modern industry ". Its downfall was inevitable. Saint-Simon's ambition was nothing less than to provide a substitute for it.

It is not, however, quite fair to lay at Saint-Simon's door all the absurdities afterwards perpetrated in his name by the Saint-Simonist sect. The literary propagation of his doctrines led to the investment of the master with a spurious halo of sanctity; and from this it was a short step to the creation of a church with priesthood and ritual and of a secular monastery at Ménilmontant, in the suburbs of Paris, in which forty of the faithful at one moment secluded themselves. The high priest of the order, Enfantin, was a colourful and masterful figure whose writings were admitted into the canon, but whose unorthodox indulgences led to the dissolution of the order by the authorities. After serving a prison sentence Enfantin migrated to Egypt. But the sect survived for thirty or forty years in France and had some following even in foreign countries, though in England it was soon to

Studies in Revolution

be eclipsed by the more sober and reputable ritual of Comte and the Positivists; and it is an odd irony of history that this posthumous apotheosis should have awaited one who strove so earnestly to establish a secular science of society.

2

THE *COMMUNIST MANIFESTO*

THE winter of 1847–48 (it is difficult to fix a more precise date for the celebration of the centenary) saw the birth of one of the capital documents of the nineteenth century — the *Communist Manifesto*. In the summer of 1847 a group consisting mainly of German craftsmen in London held the first congress of a new " Communist League ". They had been in touch with Marx, then living in Brussels, for some time; and Engels attended the congress, which adjourned to a future congress the drafting of a programme for the League. Inspired by this prospect, Engels tried his hand and produced a catechism in twenty-five questions, which Marx and he took with them to the second League congress in London at the end of November. The congress thereupon charged Marx and Engels to draft their programme for them: it was to take the form of a manifesto. Marx worked away in Brussels through December and January. The " Manifesto of the Communist Party " was published in London in German in February 1848, a few days before the revolution broke out in Paris.

The *Communist Manifesto* is divided into four parts.

Studies in Revolution

The first reviews the rise of the bourgeoisie on the ruins of the feudal system of property relations, government and morality which it destroyed; shows how " the powerful and colossal productive forces " which the bourgeoisie itself created have now grown to a point where they are no longer compatible with bourgeois property relations and bourgeois supremacy; and finally demonstrates that the proletariat is the new revolutionary class which can alone master the forces of modern industry and end the exploitation of man by man. The second part proclaims the policy of the Communist Party, as " the most progressive and resolute section of the working class of all countries ", to promote the proletarian revolution which will destroy bourgeois power and " raise the proletariat to the position of the ruling class ". The third part surveys and condemns other recent and existing schools of socialism; and the fourth is a brief tactical postscript on the relations of Communists to other left-wing parties.

A historic document like the *Communist Manifesto* invites examination from the point of view both of its antecedents and of its consequences. On the former count the *Manifesto* owes as much to predecessors and contemporaries as most great pronouncements; and the worst that can be said is that Marx's sweeping denunciations of predecessors and contemporaries sometimes mask the nature of the debt. Babeuf, who also called his proclamation a " manifesto ", had announced the final struggle between rich and poor, between " a tiny minority " and " the

16

The " Communist Manifesto "

huge majority ". Blanqui had anticipated the class interpretation of history and the idea of the dictatorship of the proletariat (the phrase was not used by Marx himself till 1850). Lorenz von Stein had written that the history of freedom, society and political order was essentially dependent on the distribution of economic goods among the classes of the population. Proudhon also knew that " the laws of political economy are the laws of history " and measured the progress of society " by the development of industry and the perfection of its instruments " ; and Pecqueur had predicted that, with the spread of commerce, " the barriers between nation and nation will be broken down " until the day when " every man becomes a citizen of the world ". Such ideas were current coin in advanced circles when Marx wrote. But neither such borrowings, nor Marx's overriding debt to Hegel's immense synthesis, detract from the power of the conception presented to the world in the *Communist Manifesto*.

To-day it is more appropriate to study the famous manifesto in the light of its hundred-year influence on posterity. Though written when Marx was in his thirtieth year and Engels two years younger, it already contains the quintessence of Marxism. Beginning with a broad historical generalization (" the history of all hitherto existing society is the history of class struggles ") and ending with an inflammatory appeal to the workers of all countries to unite for " the forcible overthrow of all existing social conditions ", it presents Marxist methodology in its fully developed form — an interpretation of

Studies in Revolution

history which is at the same time a call to action. Some passages in Marx's writings, especially at the revolutionary crises of 1848 and 1871, appear to commend revolutionary action as a good thing in itself. Some passages, both earlier and later, appear to dwell on the iron laws of historical development in such a way as to leave little place for the initiative of the human will. But these momentary shifts of emphasis cannot be taken to impair the dual orthodoxy established by the *Communist Manifesto*, where interpretation and action, predestination and free will, revolutionary theory and revolutionary practice march triumphantly hand in hand. It propounds a philosophy of history, a dogma of revolution, belief in which will take the spontaneous form of appropriate action in the believer.

The *Communist Manifesto* is thus no broadsheet for the hoardings or the hustings. Marx — and many others who are not Marxists — would deny the possibility of any rigid separation of emotion and intellect; but using the terms in a popular sense, it is to the intellect rather than to the emotions that the *Manifesto* makes its primary appeal. The overwhelming impression which it leaves on the reader's mind is not so much that the revolution is desirable (that, like the injustice of capitalism in *Das Kapital*, is taken for granted as something not requiring argument) but that the revolution is inevitable. For successive generations of Marxists the *Manifesto* was not a plea for revolution — that they did not need — but a prediction about the way in which the revolution would inevitably happen combined with a

The " Communist Manifesto "

prescription for the action required of revolutionaries to make it happen. The controversies of a hundred years ranged round the questions as to what Marx actually said or meant and how what he said should be applied to conditions diverging widely from those of his own time and place. Only the bold offered openly to " revise " Marx ; the sagacious interpreted him. The *Communist Manifesto* has thus remained a living document. The centenary of the *Communist Manifesto* cannot be celebrated otherwise than in the light, and in the shadow, of the Russian revolution which was its culminating embodiment in history.

The *Communist Manifesto* sets out a coherent scheme of revolution. " The history of all hitherto existing society is the history of class struggles." In modern times Marx detects two such struggles — the struggle between feudalism and the bourgeoisie, ending in the victorious bourgeois revolution, and the struggle between the bourgeoisie and the proletariat, destined to end in the victorious proletarian revolution. In the first struggle a nascent proletariat is mobilized by the bourgeoisie in support of bourgeois aims, but is incapable of pursuing independent aims of its own : " every victory so obtained is a victory for the bourgeoisie ". In the second struggle Marx recognizes the presence of the lower middle class — " the small manufacturer, the shopkeeper, the artisan, the peasant " — which plays a fluctuating role between bourgeoisie and proletariat, and a " slum proletariat " which is liable to " sell itself to reactionary forces ". But these

Studies in Revolution

complications do not seriously affect the ordered simplicity of the main pattern of revolution.

The pattern had been framed in the light of Marx's reading in modern English and French history and in the works of French and British economists, and of Engels's study of factory conditions in England. The English bourgeois revolution, winning its victory in the seventeenth century, had fully consolidated itself by 1832. The French bourgeois revolution, more suddenly and dramatically triumphant after 1789, had succumbed to reaction only to re-emerge once more in 1830. In both countries the first revolutionary struggle of the modern age, the struggle between feudalism and bourgeoisie, was virtually over; the stage was set for the second struggle, between bourgeoisie and proletariat.

The events of 1848, coming hard on the heels of the *Manifesto*, did much to confirm its diagnosis and nothing to refute it. In England the collapse of Chartism was a set-back which none the less marked a stage in the consolidation of a class-conscious workers' movement. In France the proletariat marched shoulder to shoulder with the bourgeoisie in February 1848, as the *Manifesto* had said it would, so long as the aim was to consolidate and extend the bourgeois revolution. But once the proletariat raised its own banner of social revolution the line was crossed. Bourgeoisie and proletariat, allies until the bourgeois revolution had been completed and made secure, were now divided on opposite sides of the barricades by the call for proletarian revolution.

The " *Communist Manifesto* "

The first revolutionary struggle was thus over : the second was impending. In Paris, in the June days of 1848, Cavaignac saved the bourgeoisie and staved off the proletarian revolution by massacring, executing and transporting the class-conscious workers. The pattern of the *Communist Manifesto* had been precisely followed. As Professor Namier, who is no Marxist, puts it : " The working classes touched off, and the middle classes cashed in on it ".

> The June revolution [as Marx wrote at the time] for the first time split the whole of society into two hostile camps — east and west Paris. The unity of the February revolution no longer exists. The February fighters are now warring against each other — something that has never happened before ; the former indifference has vanished and every man capable of bearing arms is fighting on one side or other of the barricades.

The events of February and June 1848 had provided a classic illustration of the great gulf fixed between bourgeois and proletarian revolutions.

Farther east the pattern of England and France did not fully apply, as the concluding section of the *Manifesto* admitted — almost by way of an after-thought.

In Germany the bourgeois revolution had not yet begun. The German bourgeoisie had not yet won the fundamental political rights which the English bourgeoisie had achieved in 1689 and the French a hundred years later. The task of the German proletariat was still therefore to support the bourgeoisie in the first revolutionary struggle against feudalism ; in Germany, in the words of the *Manifesto*, " the Communist Party fights with the

Studies in Revolution

bourgeoisie whenever it acts in a revolutionary manner against the absolute monarchy, the feudal landlords and the petty bourgeoisie ". But it could not be argued that Germany would simply follow the same path as England and France at a greater or less distance of time. The German revolution would occur " under the most advanced conditions of European civilization " which would give it a special character. Where the proletariat was already so advanced, thought Marx, the bourgeois revolution " can only be the immediate prelude to the proletarian revolution ".

When Marx, in the brief concluding section of the *Manifesto*, devoted to Communist Party tactics, thus announced the prospect in Germany of an immediate transition from bourgeois to proletarian revolution without the intervening period of bourgeois rule, he showed a keen historical perception, even at the expense of undermining the validity of his own theoretical analysis. The events of 1848 in the German-speaking lands confirmed Marx's intuition of the impossibility in Germany of a period of established bourgeois supremacy comparable with that which has set so strong a mark on English and French history. This impossibility was due not so much to the strength of the German proletariat, which Marx perhaps exaggerated, as to the weakness of the German bourgeoisie. Whatever the prospects of an eventual proletarian revolution in mid-nineteenth-century Germany, the material for a bourgeois revolution such as England and France had long ago achieved was still conspicuously absent.

The " Communist Manifesto "

Indeed, the bourgeoisie, far from bidding for power for itself, was plainly ready to ally itself with the surviving elements of feudalism for defence against the proletarian menace. It need hardly be added that the same symptoms, in a still more pronounced form, repeated themselves in Russia more than half a century afterwards.

The problem, therefore, which Germany presented in 1848 to the authors of the *Communist Manifesto* was the same which Russia would one day present to the theorists of her revolution. According to the revolutionary pattern of the *Communist Manifesto*, the function of the bourgeoisie was to destroy feudal society root and branch preparatory to its own destruction in the final phase of the revolutionary struggle by the proletariat. But what was to happen if the bourgeoisie through weakness or cowardice — or perhaps through some untimely premonition of its own eventual fate — was unable or unwilling to perform its essential function? Marx never provided a categorical answer to this question. But his answer was implicit in the doctrine of " permanent revolution ", which he propounded in an address to the Communist League in 1850:

> While the democratic petty bourgeoisie wants to end the revolution as rapidly as possible . . . our interests and our task consist in making the revolution permanent until all the more or less possessing classes are removed from authority, until the proletariat wins State power.

The responsibility was thus placed on the proletariat to complete the task, which the bourgeoisie had failed to perform, of liquidating feudalism.

Studies in Revolution

What form the liquidation was to take when the proletariat found itself directly confronted by a feudal society without any effective and independent bourgeoisie was not altogether clear. But if one insisted — as Marx apparently did, and Engels continued to do down to the end of his life — that " our party can come to power only under some such form as a democratic republic ", then the conclusion followed that the immediate aim of the proletariat must be limited to the establishment of a political democracy in which it was interested only as a necessary stepping-stone to the proletarian social revolution. This was, however, a theoretical construction unlikely to be realized in practice — as the experience of both the German and the Russian revolutions was one day to show. Marx never really fitted his analysis of revolution to countries where the bourgeoisie was incapable of making its own revolution; and acrimonious controversy about the relation between bourgeois and proletarian revolutions continued to divide the Russian revolutionaries for several decades.

The economic corollary of this conclusion was still more startling. If the establishment of a democratic republic was a prerequisite of the proletarian revolution, so also was the full development of capitalism; for capitalism was the essential expression of bourgeois society and inseparable from it. Marx certainly held this view as late as 1859 when he wrote in the preface to the *Critique of Political Economy*: " No social form perishes until all the productive forces for which it provides scope have

The " Communist Manifesto "

been developed ". It appeared to follow, paradoxically enough, that in backward countries the interest of the nascent proletariat was to promote the most rapid development of capitalism and capitalist exploitation at its own expense.

Such was the view seriously propounded by Russian Marxists, Bolshevik and Menshevik alike, down to 1905 — perhaps even down to 1917. Meanwhile, however, in the spring of 1905, Lenin's practical mind worked out a new scheme under which the proletariat was to seize power in conjunction with the peasantry, creating a " democratic dictatorship " of workers and peasants; and this became the official doctrine of the October revolution. The Mensheviks stuck to their guns, and their survivors and successors to-day attribute the shortcomings of the Russian revolution to its failure to pass through the bourgeois-democratic, bourgeois-capitalist phase on its way to the achievement of socialism. The issue is not to be settled by reference to Marx, who can hardly be acquitted of inconsistency on this point. Either he made a mistake in suggesting, in the last section of the *Communist Manifesto*, that Germany might pass immediately from the bourgeois to the proletarian revolution; or he failed to fit this new conception into the revolutionary framework of the earlier part of the *Manifesto*.

Marx was to encounter similar difficulties in applying the generalizations of the *Communist Manifesto* about nationalism, which were also based on British and French experience, to central and eastern

Studies in Revolution

Europe. The charge often brought against Marx of ignoring or depreciating national sentiment rests indeed on a misunderstanding. The famous remark that " the workers have no country ", read in its context, is neither a boast nor a programme; it is a complaint which had long been a commonplace among socialist writers. Babeuf had declared that the multitude " sees in society only an enemy, and loses even the possibility of having a country " ; and Weitling had connected the notion of country with the notion of property :

> He alone has a country who is a property owner or at any rate has the liberty and the means of becoming one. He who has not that, has no country.

In order to remedy this state of affairs (to quote once more from the *Manifesto*) " the proletariat must first conquer political power, must rise to be the dominant class of the nation, must constitute itself the nation, so that the proletariat is so far national itself, though not in the bourgeois sense ".

The passage of the *Manifesto* in which these sentences occur is not free from ambiguities. But the thought behind it is clear. In Marx's view, which corresponded to the facts of English and French history, nationalism grew up as an attribute of bourgeois society at a time when the bourgeoisie was a revolutionary and progressive force. Both in England and in France the bourgeoisie, invoking the national spirit to destroy a feudalism which was at once particularist and cosmopolitan, had through a period of centuries built up a centralized State on

The " *Communist Manifesto* "

a national basis. But the advance of capitalism was already making nations obsolete.

National differences and antagonisms are to-day vanishing ever more and more with the development of the bourgeoisie, free trade in the world market, the uniformity of industrial production and the conditions of life corresponding thereto.

With the victory of the proletariat they will vanish still faster. . . . With the disappearance of classes within the nation the state of enmity between nations will come to an end.

Hence the first step was for the proletariat of every country to " settle accounts with its own bourgeoisie ". The way would then be open for a true international communist order. Like Mazzini and other nineteenth-century thinkers, Marx thought of nationalism as a natural stepping-stone to internationalism.

Unfortunately the national pattern of the *Manifesto*, far from being universal, proved difficult to extend beyond the narrow limits of the place (western Europe) or the time (the age of Cobden) in which it was designed. Beyond western Europe the same conditions which prevented the rise of a powerful bourgeoisie also prevented the development of an orderly bourgeois nationalism. In central Europe (the Hapsburg Empire, Prussia) as well as in Russia the centralized State had been brought into being under pressure of military necessity by feudal overlords indifferent to national feeling; and when in the nineteenth century, under the impetus of the French revolution, nationalism became for

Studies in Revolution

the first time a force to be reckoned with in central and eastern Europe, it appeared not — as in England and France — as an attribute and complement of the State but as a sentiment independent of any existing State organization.

Moreover, the relation of nation to State worked itself out in different ways and sometimes involved even the same national group in inconsistent attitudes. This was particularly true of the Hapsburg Empire. The growing national consciousness of the German-Austrian bourgeoisie did not diminish its support of imperial unity; the bourgeoisie of the other constituent national groups sought to destroy that unity or at least to dissolve it into a federation. The Hungarians asserted the rights of the Magyar nation against the German-Austrians, but denied the national rights of Croats and Slovaks.

In these circumstances it is not surprising that Marx and Engels never succeeded in working out, even for their own day and generation, a consistent theory of nationalism which would hold good throughout Europe. They supported the Polish claim to national independence; no revolutionary, no liberal, of the nineteenth century could have done otherwise. But Engels, at any rate, seemed mainly concerned that this claim should be satisfied at the expense of Russia rather than of Prussia, proposing on one occasion to offer the Poles Riga and Mitau in exchange for Danzig and Elbing; and in the candid outburst of a private letter to Marx he referred to the Poles as " *une nation foutue,* a serviceable instrument only until Russia herself is

The " Communist Manifesto "

swept into the agrarian revolution ". In the same spirit he rejected outright the national aspirations of the Slavs of the Hapsburg Empire, whose triumph would be, in his eyes, a subjugation " of the civilized west by the barbaric east ".

In these judgments, from which Marx is not known to have dissented, Engels was indubitably swayed by national prejudice and in particular by hostility to Russia as the most reactionary Power of the day. But he was also moved by the recognition that these nationalisms of central and eastern Europe, whose economic basis was agrarian, had little or nothing to do with the bourgeois nationalism of which Marx and he had taken cognizance in the *Communist Manifesto*. It was not only a question of " the civilized west " and " the barbaric east " : it was a question of the subjugation " of town by the country, of trade, manufacture and intelligence by the primitive agriculture of Slavonic serfs ". On the presuppositions of the *Manifesto*, this seemed necessarily a retrograde step. The failure of Marx and Engels to take account of agrarian nationalism was one aspect of the other great lacuna of the *Manifesto* — the question of the peasant.

If, however, the theory of nationalism propounded in the *Communist Manifesto* could not be transplanted from western to central and eastern Europe, it equally failed to stand the test of time. The *Manifesto* contains indeed one reference to " the exploitation of one nation by another " and declares, by what seems a tautology in one sense and a *non sequitur* in another, that it will end when the exploitation

Studies in Revolution

of one individual by another ends. But Marx has little to say (nothing at all in the *Manifesto* itself) about the colonial question, touching on it in detail only in the case of Ireland; and here it is perhaps significant that, while in 1848 he was prepared to sacrifice the Irish in the same way as the Austrian Slavs, he had become convinced by 1869 that " the direct absolute interest of the English working class demands a rupture of the present connexion with Ireland ". Marx did not, however, live to see the full development of the process by which the great nations, already victims of the contradictions of capitalism, vied with one another in bringing the whole world under their yoke in a desperate attempt to save themselves and the capitalist system — the process which Lenin was afterwards to analyse in his famous work on *Imperialism as the Highest Stage of Capitalism*; nor could he foresee that rise to national consciousness of innumerable " unhistorical " nations of which the Austrian Slavs had been the harbingers. The Soviet theory of nationality, in which the colonial question and the question of small nations divide the honours between them, can derive only a pale and faltering light from the simple and far-away formulation of the *Communist Manifesto*. But critics of the national theories, whether of Marx or of the Bolsheviks, may do well to reflect that bourgeois thinkers and statesmen have also not been able to formulate, and still less to apply, a consistent doctrine of national rights.

Marx's attitude to the tiller of the soil is more seriously open to criticism. Here too there is a

The " Communist Manifesto "

foretaste of subsequent controversy — both the Mensheviks and Trotsky were accused, rightly from Lenin's point of view, of " underestimating " the peasant; and here too Marx ran into trouble because his initial theories had been primarily framed to fit western conditions. The *Communist Manifesto* praised the bourgeoisie for having, through its development of factories and towns, " delivered a great part of the population from the idiocy of country life "; and it classed peasant or peasant proprietor with handicraftsmen, small traders and shopkeepers as members of the " petty bourgeoisie " — an unstable and reactionary class, since it struggled against the greater bourgeoisie, not for revolutionary ends, but only in order to maintain its own bourgeois status. In England, in France (which in revolutionary circles was generally thought of as Paris writ large) and in Germany, the *Communist Manifesto* upheld the strict pattern of successive revolutions of which the bourgeoisie and the proletariat would be the respective driving forces, and reserved no independent place for the peasant.

Events were soon to show up the lacuna left by this scheme of things even in western Europe. The French peasants were unmoved when the revolutionary workers of Paris were shot down in June 1848 by the agents of the bourgeoisie, and voted solidly for the bourgeois dictatorship of Louis Napoleon. In fact they behaved exactly as the *Communist Manifesto* expected them to behave (which did not save them from incurring some of Marx's fiercest invective in *The Eighteenth Brumaire of Louis Napoleon*);

Studies in Revolution

but in so doing they showed how far things would have to travel before the French proletariat would be able to make another French revolution.

In Prussia and throughout Germany the revolution of 1848 was in the hands of intellectuals who thought as little of the peasants as Marx himself; and the peasants failed to move. In Austria the peasants did move. They rose in Galicia against the landlords and would have risen elsewhere with the right leadership. They formed a large and vocal group in the new democratic Reichstag. But the claims of the peasant encountered the hostility of the bourgeoisie and the indifference of the urban workers. Peasantry and proletariat were crushed separately in the absence of a leader and a programme to unite them; and in central Europe the surest moral of 1848 was that no revolution could succeed which did not win the peasant and give a high priority to his concerns.

In eastern Europe this was still more abundantly clear. As regards Poland, even the *Communist Manifesto* declared that " the Communists support the party that sees in agrarian revolution the means to national freedom, the party which caused the Cracow insurrection of 1846 ". But this passage, which occurs in the tactical postscript, is the only incursion of the *Manifesto* into eastern Europe and the only reference to agrarian revolution; and even here agrarian revolution is regarded as the ally of a bourgeois revolution leading to " national freedom ", not of a proletarian revolution.

Spending the rest of his years in England, where

The " *Communist Manifesto* "

there was no peasantry and no agrarian question, Marx never felt any strong impulse to fill this lacuna in the *Communist Manifesto*. In 1856, drawing a moral from the failure of 1848 in Germany, he spoke casually of the importance of backing up the future proletarian German revolution " with some second edition of the Peasants' War ". But even here only a subsidiary role was assigned to the peasantry. It was towards the end of his life that Marx was called on to pass judgment on a controversy just opening in far-away Russia. The leading Russian revolutionaries, the Narodniks, regarded the Russian peasant commune with its system of common tenure of land as the seed-bed of the future Russian Socialist order. On the other hand, the first Russian Marxists were already beginning to argue that the way to socialism could only lie, in Russia as elsewhere, through a development of capitalism and the proletariat.

Four times did the Marx-Engels partnership attack this ticklish issue. In 1874, before the Russian Marxists had raised their head, Engels had recognized the possibility in favourable conditions of the direct transformation of the communal system into a higher form, " avoiding the intermediate stage of individualized bourgeois property ". In 1877, in reply to an attack in a Russian journal, Marx confined himself to a doubtful admission that Russia had " the finest chance which history ever presented to a nation of avoiding the up-and-downs of the capitalist order ". In 1881 Marx gave a more positive response to a direct personal inquiry from

Studies in Revolution

Vera Zasulich; and in the following year the last and most authoritative pronouncement appeared in the preface to a Russian translation of the *Communist Manifesto*, signed jointly by both its authors:

> If the Russian revolution is the signal for a workers' revolution in the west so that these complement each other, then the contemporary Russian system of communal ownership can serve as the starting-point for a Communist development.

Russian Social-Democrats of a later generation, both Bolshevik and Menshevik, looked askance at this quasi-Narodnik deviation, and returned to the purer theoretical pattern of the *Manifesto* with its clear-cut dialectic of bourgeois and proletarian revolutions; and Lenin himself, not less than the Mensheviks, sternly maintained the paradox that the further development of capitalism in Russia was a necessary prelude to social revolution. Nevertheless, Lenin, like Marx in his later years, recognized that no revolution, and no revolutionary, in eastern Europe could afford to ignore the peasant and his demands. After 1905 — and before and after 1917 — the Bolsheviks were obliged to devote an immense amount of energy and controversy to the task of fitting the Russian peasant into the western formulae of the *Communist Manifesto*.

Franz Mehring, Marx's best and most sympathetic biographer, remarks of the *Communist Manifesto* that " in many respects historical development has proceeded otherwise, and above all has proceeded more slowly, than its authors expected ". This is true of the expectations of the two young men who

The " Communist Manifesto "

composed the *Manifesto*. But how far were these expectations modified? As regards pace, Marx in later life certainly no longer believed in the imminence of the proletarian revolution with all the eager confidence of 1848. But even the *Manifesto* in one of its more cautious passages had predicted temporary successes followed by set-backs and a slow process of " growing unity " among the workers before the goal was achieved. Marx came, with advancing years, to accept the necessity of a long course of education for the proletariat in revolutionary principles; and there is the famous *obiter dictum* in a speech of the 1870s, which admits that in certain advanced countries the victory of the proletariat may be achieved without revolutionary violence.

As regards the scheme of historical development, it would be difficult to prove that Marx, speaking theoretically and *ex cathedra*, ever abandoned the strict analysis of revolution which he had worked out in the *Communist Manifesto*. But he was not a pure theorist. He was willy-nilly the leader of a political party; and it was when he found himself compelled to make pronouncements in this capacity that he sometimes appeared to derogate from his principles. Thus in the last section of the *Manifesto* itself he had already foreseen that in Germany the bourgeois revolution would be the " immediate prelude " of the proletarian revolution, thus skipping over the period of bourgeois supremacy; in the next few years he was drawn into some uncomfortable compromises and inconsistencies on the national question; and towards the end of his life he was

35

Studies in Revolution

constrained to admit that a predominantly peasant country like Russia had the chance of achieving the social revolution without passing through the bourgeois capitalist phase at all, thus not merely modifying but side-tracking altogether the revolutionary analysis of the *Manifesto*.

It is curious and significant of the vitality of Marx's thought to watch how accurately this evolution was repeated in the Russian Social-Democratic Party. Its first leaders — Plekhanov and Axelrod, Lenin and Martov — accepted without question the scheme of the *Communist Manifesto*. After 1903 the Mensheviks, remaining consistent with themselves and with the Marxist scheme, ended in bankruptcy because they could find no way of applying it to Russian conditions. The more flexible Lenin took the scheme and brilliantly adapted it to those conditions; and the adaptations which he made followed — in broad outline, though not in every detail — those which Marx himself had admitted in his later years. The process can be justified. Marxism was never offered to the world as a static body of doctrine; Marx himself once confessed that he was no Marxist; and the constant evolution of doctrine in response to changing conditions is itself a canon of Marxism.

It is on such grounds that the Russian revolution can claim to be a legitimate child of the *Communist Manifesto*. The *Manifesto* challenged bourgeois society and offered a revaluation of bourgeois values. The Bolshevik revolution, with all its deviations, all its adaptations to specifically Russian conditions and

The " Communist Manifesto "

all the impurities which always disfigure practice as opposed to theory, has driven home the challenge and sought to apply the revaluation. That bourgeois society has been put progressively on the defensive in the past hundred years, that its fate still hangs in the balance, few to-day will deny; and until that fate is settled, until some new synthesis has been achieved, the *Communist Manifesto* will not have said its last word.

3

PROUDHON: ROBINSON CRUSOE
OF SOCIALISM

"A MAN of paradoxes" Proudhon called himself in one of his earliest extant letters in that challenging, defiant manner which is characteristic of his personality and of his style. It was no empty boast. It is the same man who can proclaim that "God is Evil" and that "Christianity has no ethic and cannot have one", but that "atheism is even less logical than faith" and that Catholicism is "the unique refuge of morality and beacon of conscience". It is the same man who declared that he voted against the constitution of 1848 not because it was a good or bad constitution, but because it was a constitution, and who praised the Vienna settlement of 1814–15 as "the real starting-point of the constitutional era in Europe". It is the same man who argued that war was irrelevant because it did nothing to solve essential economic problems, but declared that "man is above all else a warrior animal" and that "it is through war that his sublime nature becomes manifest".

Proudhon's writings are difficult of access owing both to their incoherence and to their enormous

Proudhon: Robinson Crusoe of Socialism

extent. Editors and publishers have, on the whole, been kind, and most of his major works are readily available, though a mammoth complete edition remains unfinished. The fourteen volumes of the far-from-complete collection of his correspondence have been conveniently reduced for the ordinary reader to a single volume of selections;[1] but the mass has received a fresh accretion from the recent publication of a series of important and characteristic letters from the last years of his life to his friend Rolland.[2]

There is thus ample evidence that Proudhon has retained his fascination for his countrymen, if only as a vast storehouse of ideas from which nuggets of any quality and complexion can be drawn. Many years ago Bouglé, who remains the most satisfactory of a host of commentators, neatly but inadequately ticketed him as an analyst of the social forces of revolution. To-day a volume of carefully chosen extracts from his works,[3] the tendency of which is indicated by the interlarding of the text with passages from Péguy and by a quotation from General de Gaulle on the title-page, calls for a " return to Proudhon " as the antidote to the poisons of capitalism, democracy *and* socialism, and as the symbol of a recall to religion. Meanwhile an ingenious American professor, using many of the same texts and taking the hint from a eulogy of Proudhon which appeared in the French collaborationist Press under

[1] P. J. Proudhon, *Lettres choisies et annotées*, par Daniel Halévy et Louis Guilloux.

[2] P. J. Proudhon, *Lettres au citoyen Rolland.*

[3] Proudhon, *Textes choisis*, par Alexandre Marc.

Studies in Revolution

the German occupation, depicts him with skill and plausibility as the first progenitor of Hitlerism.[1] More judicial than either of these, Mlle. Amoudruz has produced a scholarly monograph [2] which, while professedly confined to Proudhon's views on international affairs, necessarily touches on the wider ground of his whole political creed.

The element of incoherence in Proudhon derives largely from the character of the man. He had a passion for contradiction, and contradicted himself almost as readily as he contradicted others. Sometimes, especially in the letters, one suspects the practical joker. When he explains his hostility to the North in the American civil war by his dislike of "so-called liberal and democratic states" he may be nine-tenths serious (though that was not the fundamental reason for his attitude). When he adds, "J'ai en horreur la liberté", he is manifestly putting out his tongue at his correspondent and at himself. But there was in Proudhon a profound and unresolved contradiction between revolutionary opinions which expressed, in part, at any rate, his resentments against a cramped, poverty-stricken and persecuted life and the passion of the self-educated peasant for bourgeois respectability. He might, in theory, reject Church and State, authority and property. But anything that touched the sanctity of the family aroused his instinctive fury. It was this that led him into his last and most

[1] J. Selwyn Schapiro, "Pierre Joseph Proudhon, Harbinger of Fascism" (*American Historical Review*, Vol. L, No. 4, July 1945.)
[2] Madeleine Amoudruz, *Proudhon et l'Europe.*

Proudhon: Robinson Crusoe of Socialism

grotesque self-contradiction. The man who had started his career (and made his name) by declaring that property is theft, ended it by denouncing a tax on inheritance on the ground that it destroyed the family by transferring its property to the State.

The question of the influence of the Hegelian doctrine of thesis and antithesis in forming Proudhon's thought has been frequently canvassed. No thinker of the day could escape Hegel; and Herzen tells a pleasant story of Bakunin expounding to Proudhon through the whole of one night, by the embers of a dying fire, the mysteries of the Hegelian dialectic. Proudhon even wrote a long and complicated work entitled *Système des contradictions économiques ou philosophie de la misère*, in which he proved that the soundest economic principles had the most evil consequences, though all led ultimately to the goal of equality. But Marx, who indited an angry retort entitled *La Misère de la philosophie*, was probably right in alleging that Proudhon never understood Hegel. A superficial dabbling in the dialectic provided a respectable cloak for the Proudhonian passion for paradox — but little more.

There is, however, another element in Proudhon's self-contradiction which is missed by those editors and critics — unfortunately, a majority of them — who fail to place him against the rapidly changing background of his period. " I mistrust an author who pretends to be consistent with himself after twenty-five years' interval ", wrote Proudhon; and the plea is incontestably valid for the generation

Studies in Revolution

(Proudhon's dates are 1809–65) whose careers were split in two by the historical watershed of 1848. His first prolific years as a writer were passed amid the generous revolutionary enthusiasms of the 1840s — a period fertile in ideas so simple, so noble and so Utopian that it seems difficult to take them seriously to-day, yet the seed-bed of nearly all political thought for the rest of the century. Everything that was radical and subversive in Proudhon's thought grew out of this congenial soil. " Destruam et Aedificabo " was the motto which he prefixed to one of his early works. It would have been representative of his attitude at this time if he had been content to plead, like Bakunin, that " the passion for destruction is also a creative passion ".

For the visionaries of the 1840s, the year 1848 came as a bitter disillusionment. The great upheaval which was to complete the work of the French Revolution and usher in the age of social equality and the brotherhood of man had ended, in the very capital of revolution, with the shooting down of the workers by Cavaignac amid the approbation of the self-satisfied bourgeoisie and its representative assembly. The split had come between the middle class and the workers, between bourgeois democracy and " social democracy ", alias Communism. This was the lesson and the consequence of 1848. Marx drew the necessary conclusion and invented the doctrines of " the dictatorship of the proletariat " and " permanent revolution ". The proletariat must now take matters into their own hands and bring to full fruition the revolution which the bour-

Proudhon: Robinson Crusoe of Socialism

geoisie had failed to consummate. From this time forward the bourgeoisie became the target of all the worst insults of the revolutionaries. The revolt against bourgeois democracy, due to the disillusionments of 1848 and after, still determined the anti-political bias of the French syndicalist movement fifty years later.

The reaction against 1848, intersecting the Utopian idealism of his earlier years, governed the self-frustrating course of all Proudhon's subsequent thought. Like Marx, he turned violently against bourgeois democracy, and pursued its leaders into exile — Louis Blanc, Ledru-Rollin and the rest — with some of his most venomous sallies. " Democracy ", he writes in *La Solution du problème social*, " composes its ruling class (*son patriciat*) of mediocrities." Pages might be filled with arguments — or sheer abuse — from his later writings against universal suffrage, " the surest means of making the people lie ". An extract from *Les Confessions d'un révolutionnaire* echoes precisely the familiar Marxist thesis :

How could universal suffrage reveal the thought, the real thought, of the people, when the people is divided by inequality of fortunes into classes subordinate one to the other and voting either through servility or through hate; when this same people, held in restraint by authority, is incapable notwithstanding its sovereignty of expressing its ideas on anything ; and when the exercise of its rights is limited to choosing, every three or four years, its chiefs and its impostors ?

But Marx was, after all, right in describing Proudhon as a *petit bourgeois*; and he had all the

Studies in Revolution

petit bourgeois fear of, and contempt for, the proletariat (a noteworthy anticipation here of the ideological foundations of National Socialism). Picking up Saint-Simon's formula of "la classe la plus nombreuse et la plus pauvre", he declared that this class is, "by the very fact of its poverty, the most ungrateful, the most envious, the most immoral and the most cowardly"; and later he was to speak of "the stupidity of the proletariat content to work, to hunger and to serve, provided its princes grow fat and glorious".

For Proudhon, therefore, there was no escape after 1848, as there was for Marx, into the ideology of the proletariat as the bearer of the revolutionary faith. Proudhon became a revolutionary without a party, without a class, without a creed, "the Robinson Crusoe of Socialism", as Trotsky called him; and the position suited, and intensified, the wayward individualism of his temperament. The most significant analogies that can be found for his development are the Russian revolutionaries, Herzen and Bakunin. Several curious letters to Herzen appear in Proudhon's correspondence of the eighteen-fifties. Like him, Herzen had lost faith in western democracy without acquiring faith in the proletariat; and after 1855 Herzen sought to build his hopes — short-lived, indeed — on the liberal aspirations of the young Tsar Alexander II. Meanwhile Bakunin had written from a Russian prison his famous *Confessions* to Nicholas I; and in Siberia he toyed with the potentialities of enlightened despotism in the person of the Governor-General,

Proudhon: Robinson Crusoe of Socialism

Muraviev. It can hardly be mere coincidence that Proudhon should have followed the same path. His one contact with the Legitimists permits of a fairly innocent explanation, which is given at length in one of the newly published letters to Rolland. But his enthusiastic welcome of the *coup d'état* of December 2, 1851, as the embodiment of social revolution, his appeal to all republicans and socialists to rally to the banner of the Prince-President, and his subsequent flirtations with the Second Empire — punctuated, after Proudhon's usual manner, by periods of vituperation — cannot be so lightly dismissed. These political romantics of the 1840s, nourished on visions of a better world of the future, but disillusioned after 1848 both about the means of attaining this better world and about the human beings who were to inhabit it, strayed along some strange by-ways in the attempt to recapture their lost ideal.

Such were the conditions in which Proudhon became the founder of the political doctrine of anarchism, if anything so inchoate as anarchism — not a programme, it has been aptly said, but a *critique* of society — can be held to constitute a doctrine, and if so radical an iconoclast as Proudhon can be said to have founded anything. In the theory of anarchism Proudhon had William Godwin for his ancestor; in its practical advocacy he was preceded by Wilhelm Weitling, the wandering tailor from Magdeburg who, though only a few years older than Proudhon, started his missionary career at an earlier age. But it was Proudhon who

Studies in Revolution

first gave anarchism its place and its influence in nineteenth-century thought; for Bakunin, who might have ranked as a co-founder, gallantly awarded him the priority. Proudhon and Bakunin stand side by side as men who seem to have believed in revolution as a good in itself (though Proudhon, as usual, sometimes denounced even revolution), and felt it unnecessary, perhaps because they felt themselves unable, to furnish any positive definition of their goal. In this respect the successor who stands nearest to them is the syndicalist Sorel, who held that the business of doctrine is to provide an appropriate myth, whether true or not, to inspire and stimulate the forces of revolution.

Yet, notwithstanding all that has been said — and rightly said — about the self-contradictions of Proudhon and about the mood of frustration and disillusionment in which his teaching was rooted, the immense impression which he made on his contemporaries and on posterity bears witness to the vitality and sincerity of his thought. He gave to nineteenth-century political thinkers and political programme-makers something which they needed and which they greedily devoured. Out of the welter of Proudhon's writings there remain two fixed points round which he gravitates and to which he returns again and again with all his wonted pertinacity and with an unwonted consistency. These are his rejection of the State and of political power as a principle of evil, and his advocacy of " federalism " (whatever precisely that might mean) as a form of common organization for social and national groups.

Proudhon: Robinson Crusoe of Socialism

The conception of political power as a necessary evil called into existence by man's sinful nature is rooted in the Christian tradition; and the belief in an era of primitive bliss before the formation of States is common, among other thinkers, to Rousseau and Engels. But nineteenth-century anarchism, which first received form and content from Proudhon, is no mere vision of a golden age in the past or in the future. It is a creed of active rebellion against the State, which it seeks to destroy, if necessary by force. Proudhon begins in 1847 by demanding " la République, anarchie positive"; and in the last year of his life he defines anarchy more concretely as

a form of government or constitution in which the public and private conscience, formed by the development of science and right, is sufficient by itself for the maintenance of order and the guarantee of all liberties, and where consequently the principle of authority, police institutions, the means of prevention or repression, bureaucracy, taxation, etc., are reduced to their simplest expression.

Between these dates Proudhon's pages pullulate with denunciations of the State. It is " the constitutional muzzling of the people, the legal alienation of its thoughts and its initiative ". It is " that fictitious being, without intelligence, without passion, without morality, which we call the State "; and " whoever lays hands on me to govern me is a usurper and a tyrant ". Proudhon rejects altogether " this fatal theory of the competence of the State ".

But what is to be put into the void thus created? Proudhon has two answers to this question. The

Studies in Revolution

first derives from a fruitful inspiration of that queer genius Saint-Simon. Here was a man who was not an anarchist but — to use an anachronistic piece of jargon — a technocrat, believing that " les industriels " (by which he meant all concerned in the productive or distributive processes) were destined to control the State, that political power would be succeeded by economic power and " government " be replaced by " administration ". In a phrase apparently not used by Saint-Simon himself, but by his disciples, the State would become " an association of workers ". This vision, like Auguste Comte's surrealist plan for the management of " the human planet " by 14,000 bankers, seemed to presage the eventual elimination of the State; and it had the fortune to be adopted by both Proudhon and Engels, by both syndicalists and Bolsheviks. Proudhon attempted to give shape to the tempting prospect by outlining a scheme for a free credit bank based on the principle of " mutualism "; but neither contemporaries nor posterity have been induced to treat this seriously. It is only necessary to record on Proudhon's behalf this further claim to originality as one of the first crank financial reformers.

Proudhon's second answer, given in the last work published in his lifetime, which he called *Du principe fédérateur et de la nécessité de reconstituer le parti de la Révolution*, is that sovereignty rests with " the commune " — the local unit which has, in Proudhon's eyes, as natural a basis as the family. This unit he would allow to govern itself, to impose taxes on

Proudhon: Robinson Crusoe of Socialism

itself and perhaps even to legislate for itself. If Dr. Thomson, in his book on *Democracy in France*, is right in describing the French political ideal as " ranging from an extreme individualism which is tantamount to anarchism to a respect for small and intense human communities which are but the individual writ large ", then Proudhon was the very embodiment of the French ideal.

The Paris Commune reflected Proudhon's ideas and terminology; and the anarchists continued to uphold the tradition of the small community. Bakunin thought in terms of the Russian peasant commune, Kropotkin of the village community of the Middle Ages. Anarchism thus became a protest against the mass civilization of the industrial age. Its strength lay among the small craftsmen in countries where large-scale industry had not yet made important inroads — in Italy, in France, and above all, in Spain. In the First International it was the delegates from the Latin countries who were Proudhonists or Bakuninists and a constant thorn in Marx's side. Marx and the Marxists were, on the whole, right in affixing to anarchism and " anarchosyndicalism " what was to them the derogatory *petit bourgeois* label.

If the commune bears the weight of Proudhon's protest against the centralized State, it also opens the way to his other principle — federalism. He predicted that the twentieth century would be the age of federations. What precisely he meant by the term remains more than ordinarily vague. Bakunin regarded a " free federation of communes " as the

Studies in Revolution

only legitimate form of political organization. Proudhon, with his usual inconsistency, took existing States as his starting-point and approached the issue from the angle of current international affairs. He wanted federation as the basis of relations between States. But he perceived that one of the difficulties was the existing inequality between States, and thought that this, too, might be got over by the application of the federal principle, namely, by an "interior distribution of sovereignty and government". Federalism, in both senses, was "the alpha and omega of my policy ".

Here it becomes necessary to say something on the vexed question of Proudhon's attitude to nationality and nationalism. In his earlier life he was influenced by the flaming patriotism of Michelet. But he afterwards reacted strongly both against the man and against his work, and denounced the fashionable advocacy of self-determination and of the rights of nations to unity and independence. "Those who speak so much of re-establishing these national unities ", he wrote with a certain amount of prescience, "have little taste for individual liberties." The South in the American civil war had his enthusiastic support against the North because the Southerners were federalists seeking to break up an artificial Union. Alone among advanced thinkers of the period, Proudhon was bitterly opposed both to the liberation of Poland and to the unification of Italy. Poland has always been "the most corrupt of aristocracies and the most indisciplined of states "; what she needs is a

Proudhon: Robinson Crusoe of Socialism

" radical revolution which will abolish, with the great States, all distinctions of nationality, which will henceforth have no foundation ". As for " the *present* emancipation of Italy by the Cavours, the Victor-Emmanuels, the Bonapartes, the Saint-Simonians, the Jews, the Garibaldis and the Mazzinis " (a characteristic Proudhonian catalogue of anathemas), it is nothing but a " hideous mystification ". Writing in 1861, Proudhon breaks a lance with Herzen on the subject:

Do you suppose that it is through French egoism, hatred of liberty, or contempt for the Poles and Italians that I despise and distrust this commonplace of *nationality* which is going the rounds and makes so many rascals and so many honest men talk so much nonsense? For heaven's sake, my dear Bell [the name of Herzen's journal], don't be so touchy. Otherwise I shall be obliged to say of you what I said six months ago of your friend Garibaldi: great heart, but no head. . . . Don't talk to us of these reconstitutions of nationalities which are at bottom pure retrogression and, in their present form, a plaything used by a party of intriguers to divert attention from the social revolution.

Yet the charge of " French egoism " which Herzen had evidently brought against him is not altogether easy to refute. Proudhon's applications of his principles, if not the principles themselves, are always capricious; and his applications of the federal principle are not above suspicion. Proudhon had as large a measure as most Frenchmen of local patriotism: to the end of his days he liked to remember, and to remind the world, that he was a Franc-Comtois. But the suggestion of distributing French

51

Studies in Revolution

sovereignty in the name of federalism does not occur to him. On the contrary, Proudhon sometimes gave offence to foreigners — including his Belgian hosts during his period of exile in Brussels — by speaking too freely of the advantage of federation between France and her smaller neighbours. His desire to prevent the unification of Italy and to bring about the federalization of Austria-Hungary fitted in too comfortably with French national interests and French national prejudices to inspire undue confidence in the objectivity of his argument.

The case of Poland is less straightforward. It would be unfair to doubt the sincerity of Proudhon's conviction that an independent Poland would be a bulwark of opposition to the social revolution. " Poland has never had anything to offer the world but her Catholicism and her aristocracy." He can hardly have foreseen Russia's future role as an ally of France; for he died without having become conscious of the menacing prospect of German unity. But he had an illogically persistent sympathy for Russia, which may perhaps be explained by his temperamental leaning towards autocracy or by a common hatred of democratic liberalism.

Be that as it may, and even if one dismisses as a passing aberration, or explains away as a confusion of thought, his panegyric on war in *La Guerre et la paix*, a disconcerting streak of self-assertive nationalism is constantly getting in the way of Proudhon's federalism. Though an enemy of the State, one whose loyalties should in theory have been bounded by the limits of his own Franche-Comté, Proudhon

Proudhon: Robinson Crusoe of Socialism

was a good French patriot. He was one of the first socialists to illustrate in his person the impossibility, at any rate in western Europe, of a consistently international socialism. Marx constantly complained of the national prejudices of the English trade unionists and the French Proudhonists in the First International; and in Germany Lassalle had already laid the foundations of a German national socialism. " All my faith, all my hope, all my love ", wrote Proudhon, " are in Liberty and *la Patrie* "; and there is a paean of praise addressed to " la patrie, patrie française, patrie de la liberté ", which must not be exposed to the ordeal of translation, but goes far to explain why Proudhon has had admirers on the extreme Right of French politics as well as on the extreme Left:

> Commence ta nouvelle vie, ô la première des immortelles; montre-toi dans ta beauté, Vénus Uranie; répands tes parfums, fleur de l'humanité!
> Et l'humanité sera rajeunie, et son unité sera créée par toi: car l'unité du genre humain, c'est l'unité de ma patrie, comme l'esprit du genre humain n'est que l'esprit de ma patrie.

It is a sobering thought that these words were penned to celebrate Louis Napoleon's *coup d'état* which extinguished the Second Republic.

It is as difficult to assess the influence of Proudhon as to define the content of his thought. He poured out ideas in an unceasing flow; many of them were original, many of them were silly, some of them were brilliantly inspired. Though he had disciples, he cannot be said to have founded a school; for

Studies in Revolution

anarchism is, in Burke's phrase, " the dissidence of dissent ", and is, in its nature, recalcitrant to the idea of a school. Bakunin committed the superficial inconsistency of combining anarchist doctrine with the fruitful idea of a conspiratorial party, highly organized and disciplined from above; and from that moment anarchism and terrorism came to be associated in the public mind. This combination was perhaps defensible so long as the targets of attack were the agents of the detested State. But, later on, the anarchists in the Spanish civil war were to prove just as ruthless as other parties in their denial of liberty to any political opinion other than their own, and just as confident of their right and duty to eliminate opponents with the knife or the bullet. As Dostoevsky once said, the end of unlimited liberty is unlimited despotism.

Yet it was not so much this inner inconsistency as the whole social and industrial development of the period which condemned anarchism to sterility. Nineteenth-century anarchism was the philosophy of the isolated intellectual or of the small group, peasant or artisan, not of the industrial masses. At its best it was a noble and salutary protest against the centralizing and standardizing tendencies of mass civilization with its progressive encroachments on individual freedom and individual eccentricity. At its worst it was a futile and aimless quest for desperate remedies against symptoms which it failed to diagnose or understand. Both these elements, nobility and futility alike, were present in Proudhon's career and in Proudhon's thought. In the history

Proudhon: Robinson Crusoe of Socialism

of ideas, as in his own life, Proudhon remains a lonely figure — an isolated eccentric. His vision of a world of independent self-assertive individuals, each seeking and striving in perfect liberty to realize his own conception of justice, belonged to an age which was rapidly passing away. The big battalions of the industrial revolution were on the side of Marx.

4

HERZEN: AN INTELLECTUAL REVOLUTIONARY

ALEXANDER HERZEN claims attention in many capacities. He is not one of the major figures of world literature, but certainly a distinguished minor figure — one of the select company of diarists and memoir writers who continue to be read long after their own time. His autobiography and the abundant store of his surviving correspondence reveal him as a slightly incongruous and uncomfortable member of the generation of nineteenth-century romantics who worshipped at the shrine of George Sand. But his main title to fame must be as a publicist in the broad sense, a significant figure in the development both of Russian and of European political thought, a link between western Europe and the Russian revolution. Though he foreshadowed much that was to come, Herzen himself remained essentially a nineteenth-century intellectual. Born in Moscow in the year of Napoleon I's invasion of Russia, he died in Paris in the year of Napoleon III's downfall. The dividing-line in his life was the year 1847, when he left Russia with his family, never to return. The dividing-line in his thought, as in that

Herzen: An Intellectual Revolutionary

of so many of his contemporaries, was the year of revolution, 1848.

Herzen was the illegitimate son of a Russian aristocrat and a bourgeois German mother, though his upbringing was less unconventional than the bare statement of his origin suggests. From his mother he may have derived his understanding of western thought and idiom. He remains the most western and in many respects, notwithstanding his detestation of the western bourgeoisie, the most bourgeois of distinguished Russian writers. His paternal origin made him the first and most distinguished representative of the class known in Russian revolutionary history as "the conscience-stricken gentry". Herzen was thirteen at the time of the so-called "Decembrist conspiracy" — the first chapter in the long story of revolutionary movements in nineteenth-century Russia. The work of a handful of officers and small land-owners, it was crushed without difficulty and five of the ringleaders were executed. Herzen relates how, when the news of the execution reached Moscow, he stood with his friend Nick Ogarev, two years his junior, on Sparrow Hills, and the pair swore to devote their lives to the cause in which the Decembrists had suffered. Not every oath taken by schoolboys has been so accurately fulfilled.

Alexander Herzen's father, like most Russian aristocrats of his day, was a good "Voltairean", a rationalist in the French eighteenth-century mould. Alexander kept throughout life the strong stamp of his father's influence. He continued to profess

Studies in Revolution

himself a rationalist, even a cynic; and the profession was perfectly sincere. But this stratum was overlaid in him by a characteristic nineteenth-century vein of sentimental romanticism, both personal and political. This dual outlook made him a complex character. He was incapable of those straightforward enthusiasms which came so naturally and easily to his friend Ogarev or to Bakunin. He was capable — though he never quite recognized it himself — of a naïve political romanticism. But the approach to it always lay through disillusionment with current reality; and with Herzen the disillusionment generally seemed stronger than the belief. The history of his development may be read as a series of disillusionments.

The first of these disillusionments was with the Russia of Nicholas I. When Herzen entered the University of Moscow in 1829 the dreary and iron-handed repression of Nicholas's regime was at its height, and the university was one of the few places where hot-headed and intelligent young men still found an opportunity to indulge in dangerous thoughts. Advanced circles among the students fell into two groups — those who drew their revolutionary sustenance from German metaphysics and the teachings of Hegel, and those who sat at the feet of French political thinkers from Rousseau to the Utopian Socialists. Herzen, though he afterwards coined the famous aphorism which described Hegel as " the algebra of revolution ", was never a good Hegelian. The political influences that moulded him were predominantly French: he

Herzen: An Intellectual Revolutionary

was the political offspring of the ideas of 1789.

These ideas made young Herzen a political radical rather than a social reformer. It was the political oppression of the regime of Nicholas I, not the inequalities of the social and economic system, which shocked and disillusioned him and led him to idealize the liberal institutions of the west. From the vantage ground of Moscow it was not so difficult to see in the bourgeois monarchy of Louis-Philippe an exemplar of freedom and democracy. Herzen's disillusionment with his native land was completed when the Tsarist police pounced on the group of politically minded students of which he was a member and expelled them from the university and from Moscow. He spent the next three years in the provincial town of Vladimir. It was during this time that he married his first cousin Natalie, the illegitimate child of one of his father's brothers.

Through his father's influence, Alexander was eventually reinstated in the favour of the authorities and obtained a post in the Ministry of the Interior. But his political inclinations and freedom of speech again proved his undoing. In 1841 he was dismissed from his post and exiled from the capital for a year — this time to Novgorod. This experience was Herzen's final break with Russian reality. In 1846 his father's death left him the possessor of an ample fortune. In January 1847 he collected his wife and three children, his mother and several nurses, retainers and dependants — a party of thirteen in all — and left Moscow for Paris.

He travelled as fast as two post-chaises carrying

Studies in Revolution

thirteen people could be expected to travel, and was in Paris by the middle of March, after seven weeks on the road. The spirit of 1789 lived on in the Paris of Louis-Philippe. It was still the home of revolution and the Mecca of advanced political thinkers from all over Europe; it played much the same role as Moscow played in the 1920s and 1930s for the intellectuals of western Europe. Herzen has left in his memoirs an account of his emotions when he first stood on this holy ground:

> We had been accustomed to connect the word Paris with memories of the great events, the great masses, the great men of 1789 and 1793, memories of a colossal struggle for an idea, for rights, for human dignity. . . . The name of Paris was closely bound up with all the noblest enthusiasms of contemporary humanity. I entered it with reverence, as men used to enter Jerusalem and Rome.

It was the first, and not the last, enthusiasm in Herzen's career bred by rejection of a repellent reality.

It did not take Herzen many weeks to become disillusioned with the bourgeois monarchy. In the place of revolutionary ardour and passion for liberty he found in it only " a seventeen-year-old creed of crude egoism, of the unclean worship of material gain and tranquillity ". Even before leaving Russia he had described the " mercantilism and industrialism " of western Europe as " a syphilitic growth infecting the blood and bone of society ". There was now an open clash between the spacious traditions of Russian life as lived by the well-to-do Russian

Herzen: An Intellectual Revolutionary

gentry and the narrow, commercial, self-seeking habits of the liberal bourgeoisie; and this clash cut right across the neat picture which Herzen brought with him in his mind of western freedom as the antithesis of Russian despotism. It was at this moment of his first contact with the west that Herzen conceived that hatred and contempt of bourgeois democracy which played so capital a part not only in his own development, but in the whole development of Russian revolutionary thought.

But it was the revolution of 1848 which finally shaped Herzen's political course. He was in Italy when it began; and the despair of the past twelve months gave way to a short-lived mood of enthusiasm. By the time he got back to Paris early in May, however, the laurels of the revolution were already bedraggled. On May 15 a demonstration of workers at the Hôtel-de-Ville was dispersed and its leaders, including Blanqui and Barbès, arrested. " France ", commented Herzen bitterly, " is already asking for slavery. Liberty is burdensome." He was the first observer to diagnose that · strange political malady which Erich Fromm has analysed under the title *The Fear of Freedom* and described as the psychological foundation of Fascism. It is significant that the country in which Herzen diagnosed it was on the way to what may well be called the first Fascist dictatorship — the empire of Napoleon III.

On June 23 riots occurred in Paris. The Assembly proclaimed martial law, and Cavaignac

Studies in Revolution

crushed the workers. The sequel provoked the most famous passage in Herzen's memoirs:

> On the evening of June 26, after the victory over Paris, we heard regular volleys at short intervals. . . . We all looked at one another, our faces were green. . . . " Those are the execution squads " we said with one voice and turned away from one another. I pressed my forehead to the window-pane and was silent: such minutes deserve ten years of hate, a life-time of vengeance.

The year 1848 was the dividing-line in more than Herzen's life and thought. It was the moment when the bourgeoisie, having, in alliance with the nascent proletariat, got what it wanted, turned in fear against its allies, and passed over from the revolutionary to the conservative side of the barricades. It was the same story which was repeated, though with a different ending, in that other February revolution of 1917.

This was the turning-point which was responsible for Herzen's last great political disillusionment and last great act of faith. After 1848 he shed altogether his belief in the political institutions of the west. Democratic liberties were a sham, universal suffrage a trick to deceive and cajole the masses. Western society was rotten to the core. " The last word o civilization ", he wrote to Mazzini, " is revolution." So far Herzen, after 1848, followed the same road as Marx, Proudhon and Bakunin. All four shared the same attitude towards bourgeois democracy; none of them had any words for it other than those of hatred or contempt.

Herzen: An Intellectual Revolutionary

But what was to fill the void? Herzen, coming from a country where industry scarcely yet existed, could not take refuge with Marx in an all-sufficient and all-conquering faith in the proletariat. He was too rational and too critical, too orderly and too sensible, to travel the anarchist path with Proudhon and Bakunin. He could thus find no positive hope, and fell into a mood of sincere, though rather melodramatic, despair of civilization. He reverted to his discovery that men do not really want freedom, and offered a pungent comment on Rousseau's dictum that " man is born to be free — and he is everywhere in chains " :

> What would you say to a man who sadly shook his head and remarked that " fishes are born to fly and yet they eternally swim " ?

These were the years of Herzen's bitterest and profoundest disillusionment. They coincided with the years of his great personal tragedy — the unfaithfulness of his wife, the quarrel with Herwegh, the death of his wife — the period of storm and stress which ended only with his migration to England in the summer of 1852. But, though capable of nursing a romantic melancholy, he still needed a romantic faith in the future. In a vision which a century later has a prophetic ring he saw the torch of civilization being taken over by two young nations :

> I do not believe that the destinies of humanity and its future are fixed and nailed to western Europe. If Europe does not succeed in recovering herself by a

63

Studies in Revolution

social transformation, other countries will transform themselves. There are some already prepared for this movement, others which are preparing. One is known — I mean the States of North America; the other, full of vigour, also full of barbarity, is known little and badly.

Herzen's thoughts turned often at this time to the United States:

This young and enterprising people, more active than intelligent, is so much occupied with the material ordering of its life that it knows none of our torturing pains. . . . The sturdy race of English colonists multiplies exceedingly; and if it comes to the top, the people belonging to it will be, I will not say happier, but more contented. Their contentment will be poorer, more commonplace, more sapless than that which was dreamed of in the ideals of romantic Europe; but it will bring with it no Tsars, no centralization, perhaps no hunger. He who can put off the old European Adam and put on the new Jonathan, let him take the first steamer to — somewhere in Wisconsin or Kansas. He will be better off there than in decaying Europe.

But in the end it was not to America but to his own country that Herzen turned for salvation. "I have never felt more clearly than now", he writes to his Russian friends in 1851, "how Russian I am." And, looking back many years later, he records that "faith in Russia saved me when I was on the verge of moral ruin". This belief in Russia did not take the place of the old belief in revolution: it blended harmoniously with it. Russia, like the United States, was a country without a history (all the Slavs, except the Poles, "belong to geography rather than to history"); and nations without a

Herzen: An Intellectual Revolutionary

history are potentially revolutionary. Moreover, Russia is not only revolutionary but essentially socialist. The two pledges of her future greatness are " her socialism and her youth ". Herzen is not disturbed by the fact that " social revolution is a European idea ".

It does not follow that the western peoples alone are destined to realize it. Christianity was only *crucified* in Jerusalem.

And there is an odd *obiter dictum* about " communism " — a word which Marx was just bringing into use for the more systematic and authoritarian brand of socialism :

I think there is a certain basis of truth in the fear which the Russian Government is beginning to have of communism ; communism is Russian autocracy turned upside down.

Such was the position which Herzen had reached when Nicholas I died in 1855, in the middle of the Crimean War. In Russia the restraints and repressions of the thirty years' reign of an unimaginative and bureaucratic despot seemed suddenly relaxed. The first task of Alexander II was to wind up a disastrous and discreditable war. Defeat in war has often bred ambition for reform. This was the mood which prevailed in Russia during the first years of the new reign ; this was the mood in which Herzen launched his new journalistic venture in London. Those who reproach Herzen — as he was afterwards reproached — with having believed in the possibility of a reforming Tsar might recall how Proudhon

Studies in Revolution

hailed the empire of Napoleon III as the harbinger of social revolution; how Bakunin in captivity saw, or professed to see, visions of an enlightened and progressive despotism even under Nicholas I; and how Lassalle was later to make terms with Bismarck. Herzen's illusion that Alexander II could be impelled by public opinion to inaugurate in Russia an era of what he called " peaceful human progress ", though equally vain, was on the whole less ignoble.

The Bell was a monthly, or later a fortnightly, journal published in London in Russian, price sixpence, under the joint editorship of Herzen and Ogarev, Herzen being throughout the dominant partner and the driving force of the concern. Its first number appeared on July 1, 1857; and its circulation in its best period sometimes reached from 4000 to 5000, a phenomenal success at that time. It was the first uncensored Russian journal that had ever been published. Lenin, when he wrote a laudatory article on the centenary of Herzen's birth in 1912, praised Herzen for having been " the first to raise the standard of battle by turning to the masses with the free Russian word ". It sounds odd to suggest that *The Bell* was addressed to the masses. Herzen was, and always remained, an intellectual speaking to intellectuals, and he belonged to an age when politics were still the prerogative and monopoly of the well-to-do. But he was the first Russian public man to use the appeal to public opinion and the weapon of propaganda as instruments of political reform. That was the permanent significance of *The Bell* in Russian history.

Herzen: An Intellectual Revolutionary

For a time *The Bell* succeeded in pleasing nearly everyone. It pleased the westerners — the radicals of Herzen's own generation — who saw in it a striking example of progress along western lines and of the successful introduction of democratic methods of publicity and agitation into Russian political life. It pleased the Slavophils by its profession of faith in the Russian people. It pleased the now influential reformist wing of the official classes in Russia by strengthening their hand against the reactionaries; and by that kind of unavowed toleration which sometimes mitigated the absurdities of the Russian bureaucracy, copies of *The Bell* found their way through the censorship into high places in Russia itself. It even pleased the Emperor, who was flattered by the portrait of himself as an ardent reformer endeavouring to carry out an enlightened programme in the teeth of obstruction from old-fashioned bureaucrats.

The creation of *The Bell* was Herzen's major achievement. It would be agreeable to attribute some share in it to the country where he had taken up his abode. But the evidence reveals little trace of English influence in Herzen's life and thought. Victorian England treated the political refugee from Europe with complete toleration so long as he did not break the law, but also with complete indifference. Herzen appreciated the toleration, and was even able to praise what he called the " rude strength " and " unbending obstinacy " of the English character. He liked Colman's mustard and English pickles; and a recent Russian writer on Herzen

67

Studies in Revolution

notes his admiration for *Punch* as a satirist of English bourgeois life, and records some hitherto undetected borrowings.

But he found nothing to stimulate him, and never revised the verdict, penned three years after his arrival in London, that " life here is about as boring as that of worms in a cheese ". In a period of thirteen years he made one or two English political acquaintances — Carlyle among them — but no English friends. The role of England in his political development was purely negative. As in his youth he had lived in Russia and believed passionately in the freedom and democracy of the west, so now, in his maturity, residence in England nourished a fervent faith in the political destinies of a regenerated Russia. Herzen's enthusiasms always flourished in isolation from the realities to which they related.

The liberation of the serfs in 1861 was a Russian landmark comparable to the landmark of 1848 in western Europe, and had similar results. By liquidating the system of feudal ownership it brought Russia ostensibly into line with the west and paved the way for industrialization. By satisfying the aspirations of the Russian liberals, it turned them into conservatives; and it created a new generation of irreconcilable revolutionaries who would have no truck with mere reformers. *The Bell* could no longer hold a middle course. Herzen faltered and was caught between the two fires. Both extremes seemed to him wrong; he became, as Marx said of the Prussian bourgeoisie, " revolutionary against the conservatives, but conservative against the revolu-

Herzen: An Intellectual Revolutionary

tionaries ". Stultified by this uncertainty, *The Bell* declined rapidly from the high-water mark of 1861. The Polish insurrection of 1863 was its death-blow. Herzen had already antagonized the revolutionaries. He now antagonized the remaining moderates by espousing the Polish cause. In 1865 he moved *The Bell* to Geneva without reviving its fortunes; and it expired in 1868. Herzen himself died in Paris, a tired and — for the last time — disillusioned man, in January 1870.

If it is necessary to define in a single phrase Herzen's place in the history of the Russian revolution, he may be called " the first Narodnik ". The Narodniks formed the first generation of active Russian revolutionaries who, before Marx had made any impact on Russia, proclaimed the revolutionary potentialities of the downtrodden Russian peasant and sought salvation in the movement which came to be known as " going to the people "; and they were the direct ancestors of the Social-Revolutionaries who became the revolutionary rivals of the Marxist Social-Democrats. Herzen was the inventor of the Narodnik belief that the traditional Russian peasant community, with its undivided communal property, was a proof of the socialist character of the Russian tradition. As early as 1850 he attacked the view of the Prussian traveller Haxthausen, who had described the commune as being despotically ruled by its president and as an instrument of the imperial authority.

It was this allegedly democratic and socialist character of the Russian commune which helped

Studies in Revolution

Herzen to rationalize his faith in Russia as the pioneer of social revolution. Thanks to this, Russia could achieve socialism without having to pass through the repulsive stage of bourgeois capitalism which had wrought such havoc in western Europe. Herzen was the progenitor of the whole Narodnik (and afterwards Social-Revolutionary) doctrine, of which the cult of the Russian people, hatred of the western bourgeoisie and contempt for the western proletariat were the distinguishing features. Even Marx towards the end of his life cautiously admitted, under pressure from the Narodniks, that the existence of the Russian commune might, in certain circumstances, enable Russia to make the direct transition from feudalism to socialism without the intervening capitalist stage.

If, however, the Narodniks owed much to Herzen in the shaping of their doctrine, they emphatically rejected his belief in the possibility of peaceful evolution. This belief Herzen also justified on the ground of the socialist character of the Russian commune; for "what in the west can be achieved only through a series of catastrophes can develop in Russia on a basis of what already exists". His last political utterance is a series of open letters *To an Old Comrade*, written in 1869. The " old comrade" was Bakunin. Bakunin in his later years idealized the Russian peasant as romantically as Herzen himself and believed as firmly as Herzen in the socialist tradition of the Russian peasant commune. But Bakunin was a lifelong believer in revolution by violence; and it is on this ground

Herzen: An Intellectual Revolutionary

that Herzen now takes him to task. Herzen's condemnation of violence and terrorism was the dividing-line which separated him from the younger revolutionary generation and ranged him more and more during his last years in the conservative camp.

Before Herzen died, the cause which he had so brilliantly sustained in *The Bell* was irretrievably lost. In his own country the prospects of the revolution by persuasion which had seemed possible in the first years of Alexander II had faded away; the revolutionaries and the government were equally committed to policies of violence. The ineffectual conclusion of Herzen's career reflected, as Lenin said, " that world historical epoch when the revolutionism of bourgeois democracy was already dying and the revolutionism of the socialist proletariat had not yet ripened ". The revolution of the intellectuals in which Herzen believed had already exhausted itself; the revolution of the masses which was about to begin was one that he neither believed in nor understood. He was a revolutionary only in ideas, not in action. But his thought was a necessary step in the development of the Russian revolution; and it is pleasant to record that his qualities have lately received full and wide recognition in his own country, where the seventy-fifth anniversary of his death was commemorated by a spate of articles and other publications in 1945.

5

LASSALLE MEETS BISMARCK

GEORG BRANDES opens his essay on Lassalle, originally published in the 1870s, with some reflections on the " surprise and astonishment " provoked by " the process by which the Germany of Hegel was transformed into the Germany of Bismarck ", and notes the " strongly marked " figure of Lassalle as one of the significant features of the transformation. Ferdinand Lassalle lived for less than forty years; of his writings only the letters and diaries now possess more than an antiquarian interest; and the General German Workers' Association, which he founded, was reshaped after his death by rivals eager to consign his name and tradition to oblivion. Yet his career touched history at so many points, reflected and transmitted so many influences and foreshadowed so much that lay in the future that it remains one of the most rewarding quarries for the student of nineteenth-century political and social evolution in western Europe.

But that is not all. Ever since Meredith made a drama out of his sensational death, Lassalle has been more often remembered, at any rate in this country, for his vivid and tempestuous personality

Lassalle meets Bismarck

than for his political achievement. Mr. Footman's book, as its needlessly banal title suggests,[1] belongs to the personal rather than to the political school of biography. It is more concerned to portray Lassalle the man than to determine his place in history. It is none the less a scholarly work, written with scrupulous regard to the evidence and with a restraint which enhances its interest. It is also the first English life of Lassalle, though there is an English translation of the standard German biography by Oncken, unfortunately abridged as well as made from an early and now out-dated edition.

Born in Breslau in 1825, son of a fairly prosperous Jewish merchant one generation removed from the Polish ghetto, Ferdinand Lassal (the longer form of the name was an elegant invention of his own, dating from a visit to Paris) entered the University of Berlin at the age of nineteen, soon after Marx, Engels and Bakunin had left it. It was still in the full glow of that remarkable period when philosophy was the only study for an intelligent and ambitious young man, and Hegel (who had died in 1830) the only philosopher. Already at Breslau young Ferdinand had become a Hegelian. By this conversion he had been " born again "; and, as he explained in a long epistle to his father, " this second birth gave me everything, gave me clarity, self-assurance . . . made of me self-containing intellect, that is self-conscious God ".

The hyperbole is characteristic of the writer's

[1] David Footman, *The Primrose Path.* A Life of Ferdinand Lassalle. The Cresset Press. 15s.

73

Studies in Revolution

temperament. But it is characteristic also of the age. If the standard of measurement be the weight, the breadth and the duration of the influence which he exercised, Hegel was beyond question the most important of modern philosophers. He moulded the thought of more than one generation, and his teaching was the philosophical cradle of every significant political theory for a century to come. It was his astonishing achievement to provide within the limits of a single coherent system both a creed of State worship and an " algebra of revolution ". From 1840 onwards the " Hegelian Left " had taken the bit between its teeth and, by a strictly logical process of interpretation, made of " the master " — what he himself had certainly never dreamed of — a revolutionary standard-bearer. It was primarily in this sense that the young Lassalle became a Hegelian. But he lacked Marx's rigid consistency and (after his early student years) Marx's application; he was an agitator and pamphleteer rather than a thinker; and, as his later development showed, he had imbibed elements of the Hegelian doctrine which were anathema both to Marx and to Bakunin.

"Man's temperament is his fate", quotes Mr. Footman from his hero on the title-page; and beyond doubt Lassalle's career owed more to his temperament than to his philosophy. At the beginning of 1846 he fell in love with the beautiful but impecunious Countess Sophie von Hatzfeldt, long separated from a wealthy but mean husband and in the throes of a perennial dispute with him about

Lassalle meets Bismarck

money matters. Lassalle was twenty, and she was just twice his age. He became her mentor, legal adviser, knight errant and lover; for, even if documentary evidence is lacking, it is surely pedantic to observe Mr. Footman's cautious suspension of judgment on this last point. The Countess Hatzfeldt was the main formative and stabilizing influence in Lassalle's life, and emerges as perhaps the one wholly sympathetic figure in his biography. "She is my own re-embodied Ego", he wrote fifteen years later to one of his many mistresses; "she is part of all my triumphs and perils, fears and toil, sorrows, strains and victories, part of all the emotions I have ever had. She is the first and essential condition of my happiness."

The course of the Hatzfeldt affair was oddly intertwined with the 1848 revolution. At the moment when Louis-Philippe was being driven from France, Lassalle was arrested on the charge of instigating the theft of a casket supposed to contain vital papers belonging to the Count, and remained in prison till his trial in August. He used the dock for an eloquent recital of the Countess's grievances against her husband. By skilfully identifying her cause with that of liberty and democracy he won from a politically minded jury his own acquittal, which was not unjustly hailed as a triumph of the Left. He plunged into political agitation, and was arrested in November on a charge of inciting to violence. He did not emerge again until July 1849 (this time after a six months' sentence); and by then the revolution was over.

Studies in Revolution

The indirect result of Lassalle's prison experiences was to keep him out of any direct participation in revolutionary disturbances. He was the one Prussian revolutionary of any consequence who was not seriously compromised, and was able to remain on Prussian soil after the *débâcle* of 1849. Thus, through the reactionary period of the 1850s, he was uncontested leader of what remained in Germany of a workers' movement. When the political ice began to melt in the next decade, he became the founder in 1863 of the first embryonic German Labour Party — the General German Workers' Association. The last two years of his life made Lassalle a political figure of the first importance.

That such a man should clash with Marx for the headship of the German workers' movement was inevitable. Personal rivalries and temperamental incompatibility counted for much. Here sympathies will not be wholly on the side of Marx. Marx was an intensely jealous man, and Lassalle's relative affluence, his eloquence and the magnetic personality which won him so large a personal following, were all more than his rival could stomach. Lassalle was capable of an impulsive generosity of thought and deed which was not in Marx's nature; and he never bore malice or nourished personal enmities. That Lassalle found time for wide human and intellectual interests — including the writing of a five-act historical drama in blank verse — was not as serious a blemish on his character as it seemed to Marx's one-track mind.

On the other hand, it could not be denied that,

Lassalle meets Bismarck

as a leader of the workers, Lassalle was highly vulnerable and that many of Marx's shafts were well aimed. The intimate connexion between the wrongs of the proletariat and the Hatzfeldt *cause célèbre* was less apparent to others than to Lassalle and the Countess. When at last in 1854, through Lassalle's persistence, the Count was partly browbeaten, partly blackmailed, into making a favourable settlement on the Countess, Lassalle received out of the proceeds the tidy pension of 4000 thalers a year, and thereafter, with a sumptuous flat in Berlin, combined the life of a proletarian leader with that of a Don Juan and man about town. The second role often seemed nearer to his heart than the first. He confessed to " a horror of workers' deputations where I always hear the same speeches and have to shake hard, hot and moist hands ". Marx might have said the same ; but what would have been intellectual fastidiousness in Marx was a cultivated social snobbishness in Lassalle. The crowning tragedy in which, in his fortieth year and at the height of his political reputation, he was killed in a duel at Geneva by a young Wallachian count, his rival for the hand of a girl of 17, was the culminating instance of this constant intrusion of disreputable melodrama into his political ambitions. Others besides Marx found Lassalle's behaviour incongruous and distasteful; the reader of Mr. Footman's unimpeachably impartial story will have ample material on which to base his own judgment.

It may, of course, be said that Lassalle's flamboyant temperament, for all its restlessness and

77

Studies in Revolution

rebelliousness, had in it a marked conservative streak. Certainly he had a sense of personal property and of the value of money (he was a constant speculator on the stock exchange) which was unthinkable to Marx or Bakunin. In the affair with the Countess Hatzfeldt he revealed both a keen eye to the main chance and an unconcealed liking for high society; and neither of these tastes altered with advancing years. These things are not commonly associated with a revolutionary outlook. Few of those with whom he associated in his later years shared his proletarian sympathies. More important was the dictatorial strain in Lassalle's character. His self-assurance, his amazing vitality, his lust for power and fame, his contempt for the common man — all these seemed, at the period of history to which he belonged, to deny him any natural affinity with the political Left.

It would, however, be superficial to dismiss the rift between Marx and Lassalle as an affair of personal or political rivals between whom temperament and circumstance had fixed an unbridgeable gulf of incompatibility. To take such a view would be to underestimate Lassalle's influence and significance — a mistake which, incidentally, Marx himself did not make. It may well be argued that in the history of nineteenth- and twentieth-century Germany Lassalle proved eventually a more potent force than Marx; and the conceptions for which he stood made their way, even in countries where he exercised no direct influence at all. He was one of the first protagonists and instruments of a historical

Lassalle meets Bismarck

process which has not yet fully worked itself out — the alliance between socialism and nationalism.

Any serious analysis of the clash between Lassalle and Marx or of the ultimate significance of Lassalle as a representative historical figure must start from the divergent strands in the Hegelian system, which, from the earliest moment, appear side by side in Lassalle's thought. The historical process, ever in flux and continually advancing through a dialectical series of contradictions resolving themselves in a new synthesis — all this young Lassalle eagerly digested and, like his contemporaries, made it the basis of a passionate belief in the social revolution. Already as a student in Berlin he was exposing the "formal" and "individual" character of the liberties won by the French revolution and asserting the necessity of a new revolution to overthrow capitalism and the competitive system as the road to the liberation of the working class. This path he travelled as whole-heartedly, and as early, as Marx himself.

But, equally at this early stage, we find in Lassalle unmistakable traces of the Hegelian doctrine of the State as the foreordained institution through which alone the individual can achieve the rational development of personality and freedom. The socialist tradition, handed down from More through Godwin to Saint-Simon, and thence to Marx as well as to Proudhon and Bakunin, to Lenin as well as to Kropotkin, was fundamentally hostile to the State. The only difference on this point between Marx and Lenin on the one hand and the anarchists on

Studies in Revolution

the other was that the former accepted the State (in the form of the dictatorship of the proletariat) as a temporary, but necessary, evil until the communist society had been fully established, while the anarchists would not agree to palter even temporarily with the iniquities of State power.

For this tradition, with its belief in the dying away of the State as the ultimate goal, Lassalle was too good a Hegelian to have any sympathy whatever; and as the years went on he came more and more to regard the State as the potential instrument through which the wrongs of the workers could be redressed and the aims of socialism attained. He attacked the bourgeois State not, like Marx, because it was strong and oppressive, but because it was weak and futile. His was the famous phrase of contempt for the "night-watchman State", coined in a speech of 1862 which he published as *The Workers' Programme* :

> Thus the middle class conceives the moral object of the State. This object consists simply and solely in securing the personal freedom of the individual and his property. This is the night-watchman theory, for this conception can regard the State only under the form of a night-watchman whose duties are confined to preventing burglary and theft.

And a little later he was informing an audience of working men in terms which were the very negation of all that Marx had ever taught: "The State belongs to you, the needy classes, not to us the well-to-do, for the State consists of you ".

Lassalle's view of the State is reflected in his

Lassalle meets Bismarck

view of law, to which he devoted intensive, though intermittent, study. He defined law in Hegelian terms as an expression of the national consciousness of right. Since that consciousness varies from time to time, so also the law must vary; and on this thesis Lassalle founded a somewhat perverse argument to justify retroactive legislation. But national consciousness also varies from nation to nation, and this consideration brings Lassalle near in spirit and intention to the famous German school of jurisprudence. Indeed, the most significant aspect of Lassalle's acceptance of the State was that it involved him, perhaps unwittingly at first, in the acceptance of orthodox national patriotism, of loyalty to the national State. It is not without importance that Lassalle, almost alone among the revolutionary leaders of the nineteenth century, was never an exile and spent the whole of his working life in his own country.

Be this as it may, Lassalle by the last few years of his life had achieved an unexpected, and at this time highly original, synthesis between his socialism and his feelings as a good Prussian. The war of 1859 between France and Austria had led him to demand that Prussia should seek compensation by annexing Schleswig-Holstein. In the early 1860s he " hoped and believed " that " external factors, *e.g.* war ", would bring about the " national-political revolution " of the unification of Germany; but he added that the bourgeoisie was incapable of realizing this revolution, which would " only be effective if driven on by a solid and class-conscious

Studies in Revolution

workers' party ". In 1862 he delivered in Berlin, at the celebration of the Fichte centenary, a laudatory lecture on Fichte as a great German patriot and the prophet of German unity.

The stage was now set for the final episode of Lassalle's political career — his meetings with Bismarck. A certain piquancy is added to the situation by a letter of some two years earlier to the Countess Hatzfeldt, in which Lassalle had called Bismarck " a reactionary Junker from whom one can only expect reactionary measures ", a man who would " rattle his sword to get the military budget through on the pretence that war is imminent ". Until the 1920s the principal authority for these meetings was a statement made in 1878 by Bismarck himself in response to an interrogation in the Reichstag. This statement left it in doubt exactly when they took place and on whose initiative. Letters and other documents now available date the first meeting in May 1863, at the moment when the General German Workers' Association was being constituted, and show that the invitation came direct, without any preliminary contacts, from Bismarck himself. This discovery partially relieves Lassalle of the charge afterwards levelled at his memory by his rivals of having deliberately sought to ingratiate himself with the ruling powers. But it also assigns to Bismarck rather than to Lassalle the stroke of genius which perceived a bond of common interest between them capable of being exploited to their mutual advantage. It may also be recalled that when, some years later, Marx received similar, though less direct,

Lassalle meets Bismarck

approaches from Bismarck, he refused to be drawn into the net.

The outward link between Bismarck and Lassalle was their common hostility to the Progressives — the Prussian Liberal Party. Bismarck, who still feared them as his chief opponents, would gladly have seen their more radical elements attracted away from them by a new party of the Left; Lassalle nourished the same ambition. But the more intimate link of a common outlook on political realities drew the two men together and gave them at any rate an intellectual respect for each other. Both despised the flabby idealism and constitutional word-spinning of the Progressives; both understood that politics mean power, and they could measure their forces against each other in the same terms. Both had a fundamental contempt for democratic methods, and believed firmly in efficient dictatorship as a principle and in their own capacity to exercise it. A letter from Lassalle in the last year of his life on the affairs of the General German Workers' Association shows that he had nothing to learn from Bismarck about the imposition of his will on his subordinates:

Branch representatives are there to direct their branches as instructed by headquarters — not to take orders from the branches. . . . Whenever I attended branch meetings there was never any idea of the branch passing a resolution unless I myself took the initiative. . . . Why is it being allowed to happen otherwise in Berlin? I suppose because there one is nearer to the heart of parliamentarianism.

Studies in Revolution

Out of the soil prepared by these coincidences of interest and outlook grew that working alliance between Bismarck's nationalism and Lassalle's socialism — the " social-service State " or " State socialism " — which was Bismarck's specific contribution to domestic policy. Exactly what passed between them when they met, exactly how much Bismarck was influenced by what did pass, cannot be known. Even the number of meetings is a matter of guesswork : Bismarck himself, fifteen years later, mentioned " three or four ", the Countess Hatzfeldt " twenty ". The records show that Lassalle pressed for universal suffrage ; and Bismarck's subsequent adoption of it can hardly be dissociated altogether from his pleadings. It is certain that, at Lassalle's instigation, Bismarck caused the King to receive a deputation of Silesian weavers and to promise them consideration of their grievances. Lassalle was acute enough to guess that Bismarck " wanted to put through the social part of our programme, but not the political part ". What he did not foresee was that Bismarck, having been astute enough to " dish " the socialists by stealing the more harmless and practical trappings of their programme, would one day be strong enough to take repressive measures against the party itself.

Whatever their immediate influence, the meetings were a historical landmark. The coming together of the masterful Prussian Prime Minister and the headstrong socialist agitator symbolized the new and pregnant alliance between nationalism and socialism.

Lassalle meets Bismarck

Lassalle was by this time a patriotic Prussian as well as a sincere socialist; and it was a result of his policy that henceforth — and not in Prussia alone — a man could profess himself a good socialist and a good patriot. The national State was to become an instrument promoting, within the limits of the capitalist system, the welfare of the masses; in return the masses would become imbued with patriotic loyalty to the national State. Both these unspoken terms of the alliance were significant. If the Bismarck-Lassalle conversations foreshadowed the social-service State, they also foreshadowed the birth of " jingoism " (the word was coined in the 1870s) and sharpened the edge of nationalism by making it an interest of the masses as well as of the middle class. The field of international discord was now conterminous with the whole nation. The way was open for the coming not only of the totalitarian State, but of total war.

The creation of national, as opposed to international, socialism was, whether he consciously sought it or not, Lassalle's main historical achievement. But other striking pointers to the future may be found scattered throughout his writings and speeches. In one of his early letters to his father he foretold that the growth of industry must entail " the negation of the principle of property " and the " merging of man's subjective individuality " in the organized State. He may well have been the first to use — at any rate, he used it in the early 'sixties — the now well-worn argument that, since the State knows no financial limit to what it can spend in

Studies in Revolution

war, it can afford to spend without limit for social purposes in peace. His proposal to organize, in the place of trade unions, "productive unions" supported by the State, was a foretaste of the almost exactly similar proposal which was made by Trotsky in the early 1920s and which, though then rejected, helped to mould the future shape of the Soviet trade unions — and perhaps of others. Lassalle was not a profound or systematic thinker. His treatises on law and economics, for all their pretentiousness, are the work of a clever dilettante, not of a master of his subjects. But he had an uncanny aptitude for discerning the significant development or the significant idea — or rather the development or idea which would one day become significant. In many respects it is easier to-day than it would have been fifty years ago to recognize how far he was in advance of his time..

The period following Lassalle's death seemed to spell the defeat of nearly everything for which he stood. Six weeks after the fatal duel in Geneva, Marx brought to birth in London the International Working Men's Association — the First International. In Germany Marx's followers steadily undermined the Lassallean tradition; and when the United Social Democratic Party was at length founded in 1875, Lassalle's General German Workers' Association was merged in it without leaving more than superficial traces on its programme and leadership. Socialism had been established on a solid international basis; and Bismarck's legislation against the socialists seemed to mark the

Lassalle meets Bismarck

final breakdown of the alliance which he and Lassalle had once conspired to forge. Yet the sequel showed that, beneath all these appearances, Lassalle had builded better than he knew and that history was on his side. In 1914 it was national, not international, socialism which emerged triumphant in every European country except Russia. In Germany it was not only Bernstein the "revisionist" but Kautsky the "renegade" who showed, when the test came, that they were successors of Lassalle rather than of Marx; and without seeking to saddle the Jew from Breslau with responsibility for Hitler's particular brand of "national socialism", the curious may still speculate how far "socialism in one country" is not, in another context, an unconscious tribute to the vitality of the Lassallean conception.

6

SOME NINETEENTH-CENTURY RUSSIAN THINKERS

RUSSIAN social and political thought in the nineteenth century is of high interest and importance on two counts. It inspired one of the great creative periods of modern literature; and it forms the background of the Russian revolution of 1917. Its significance in the second context has been increased by the recent tendency to dwell on the continuity of Russian history before and after the revolution rather than on the break in continuity which was the theme of the first revolutionary writers and historians.

Shortly before the first world war T. G. Masaryk, the future president of the Czechoslovak Republic, published a detailed survey of Russian nineteenth-century thought which was translated into English in 1919 under the title *The Spirit of Russia*. But, while numerous articles have been written about individuals or particular movements, no further synoptic view of the whole field seems to have been attempted in any language till the publication in Paris in 1946 of Berdyaev's *The Russian Idea*, which has since appeared in a welcome English

Some Nineteenth-Century Russian Thinkers

translation. Berdyaev was one of a group of young Russian intellectuals who, having passed through the school and discipline of Russian Marxism, went over about 1908 to the Orthodox Church. Some time after the Bolshevik revolution he emigrated to Paris where he died in 1948. His book is slighter, more personal and more dogmatic than that of the liberal Masaryk. But, like all his work, it displays an always fresh and acute, though sometimes rather wilfully one-sided, insight into Russian conditions and ways of thought, past and present.

Russian nineteenth-century thought revolves unceasingly round the central idea of revolution. It was Nicholas I — so far as responsibility can be assigned to any one person — who, by virtually proscribing all forms of political, social and philosophical speculation, threw the whole intellectual movement of three generations into a revolutionary mould. The first overt act was the trivial " Decembrist conspiracy " of 1825 — a sort of officers' mutiny; its promoters were the first representatives of the so-called " conscience-stricken gentry ", who illustrated the perennial truth that the seeds of revolution are sown when a ruling class loses its belief in its right to rule. This stage of the movement developed under the predominant influence of Hegel. It culminated in the 'forties in the brilliant figures of Bakunin and Herzen, the first Russian revolutionary *émigrés*, who not only mediated western ideas to Russia, but also, though somewhat later, broke fresh ground by introducing Russian ideas to the revolutionary movements of western Europe.

Studies in Revolution

In Russia itself Belinsky was the most significant representative of the "men of the 'forties". Belinsky shifted the focus of the revolutionary movement from the " conscience-stricken gentry " to the middle-class intelligentsia of which he was the forerunner and creator. Though much of his comparatively brief period of literary activity was occupied by incessant controversy about the interpretation of Hegel (one of the guises in which political speculation might still hope to escape the censor's vigilance), he made the transition from the idealism of Hegel to the materialism of Feuerbach. Himself dying in 1848 in his thirty-seventh year, he paved the way for the new generation of the 'sixties and set the revolutionary movement. on a materialist basis which was not thereafter challenged.

It was the "men of the 'sixties " — Chernyshevsky, Dobrolyubov and Pisarev are generally named as the most important and typical of them — who began to give to the revolution the shape in which it ultimately triumphed. Like Belinsky, they were obliged to couch their ideas in the form of philosophical or literary criticism, and were contributors to those solid " advanced " periodicals to which the relaxed censorship of Alexander II offered a temporary and much qualified licence of opinion. Chernyshevsky, who won laudatory appraisals both from Marx and from Lenin, has been much studied in revolutionary Russia. A collected edition of his works in ten volumes appeared before the war ; and his novel *What is to be Done?* published in 1864, the year in which he was condemned for subversive

Some Nineteenth-Century Russian Thinkers

activities and sent to Siberia, is still a revolutionary classic. Dobrolyubov, a collaborator of Chernyshevsky who died prematurely in 1861, was noted for his attacks on the liberal bourgeoisie, who hoped that reform might provide an alternative to revolution (Chernyshevsky and his followers afterwards had a famous quarrel with Herzen on this issue). Pisarev, the third and most daring of the trio, won his spurs by a striking review of Turgenev's *Fathers and Sons*. While other advanced critics denounced its " nihilist " hero Bazarov as a malicious caricature, Pisarev hailed him as the true prototype of the modern revolutionary materialist. A vigorous and — considering that more than four of his twenty-eight years were spent in prison — incredibly prolific publicist, Pisarev has been made the subject of an immensely detailed monograph by a French critic, M. Armand Coquart. This is one of those meritorious and valuable works which, being devoted to a minor writer, will henceforth save all but the most meticulous from the labour of consulting the original texts, and which, once done, need never be repeated.

The " men of the 'sixties " opened the way for the active revolutionaries of the following decade. Chernyshevsky was the first revolutionary publicist to participate actively in one of the new secret societies just beginning to spring up. In the 'seventies the movement passed from the sphere of philosophy and literature to that of action, whether in the form of missionary work among the peasants (the so-called " going to the people ") or of terrorist conspiracies. The latter policy reached its climax

Studies in Revolution

with the assassination of Alexander II by Zhelyabov and his group in 1881.

The revolutionary movement was now ripe for its last stage. Hitherto every Russian revolutionary had assumed that, in an agricultural country like Russia, the peasantry must ultimately be the backbone of the revolution. But by the beginning of the 1880s the campaign of " going to the people " had failed to stir the peasant, and terrorism had been defeated by popular apathy and police repression. A new start was required. It was twenty years since the emancipation of the serfs had started the process of the industrialization of Russia with foreign capital. In 1883 Plekhanov founded the first Russian Marxist group and planted the roots of Marxism in the new industrial proletariat of Russia. The last considerable social and economic essay of the century was Lenin's maiden work, *On the Development of Capitalism in Russia*, which set out to prove that Russia was treading the western path of bourgeois capitalism on the way to proletarian revolution.

" Independent Russian thought ", writes Berdyaev, " was awakened by the problem of the philosophy of history. It had reflected deeply upon what the thoughts of the Creator were about Russia, about what Russia is and about what sort of destiny it has." Such passages, as well as the very title of his book, show that Berdyaev embraces a kind of national mysticism — a sense of the destiny of Russia as the explanation of her history — which seems to be bound up with his acceptance of Orthodox Christianity. He does not even eschew the

Some Nineteenth-Century Russian Thinkers

cruder forms of national determinism, as when he describes Lenin as " a characteristically Russian man with an admixture of Tartar traits ". This approach will invalidate some of his conclusions for those who do not share it, but does little to detract from the value of his searching analysis of the main issues which exercised Russian nineteenth-century thought.

The issue which lay beneath all others and was, in some sense, the distillation of them all was the question of Russia and Europe, of east and west, of Slavophils and westerners. After Peter the Great no Russian thinker could evade this issue. In its nineteenth-century form it was posed by Chaadaev, who declared that Russia had neither history nor tradition nor civilization of her own. Russia formed a blank in the " moral world order ".

We belong to the number of nations who so to speak do not enter into the framework of mankind and exist only in order to give the world some serious lesson.

The " men of the 'forties " all assumed without question that salvation could be found by Russia only through borrowing and assimilating from the west; nor did the " men of the 'sixties " differ from them on this vital point.

The Slavophil movement started in the 'forties as a reaction against the prevailing orthodoxy of the westerners. It indulged in an unhistorical idealization of the past, and had puerilities and affectations, extending even to matters of dress. But in the hands of Kireevsky and Khomyakov, its ablest and most

Studies in Revolution

consistent expositors, it became a powerful body of doctrine. Its essential tenets were that Russia had a tradition and civilization of her own entirely independent of those of the west; that Russia was called on to follow her own line of development, not to borrow from the west; and that the future belonged not to decadent Europe but to young and unspoiled Russia, what was commonly referred to as Russia's " backwardness " thus becoming a positive asset.

A mistake commonly made about the controversy between westerners and Slavophils is to equate westerners with radicals and revolutionaries and Slavophils with conservatives and reactionaries. There was a western conservative, as well as a western radical, tradition: Chaadaev, for example; though an out-and-out westerner, was not in any sense a radical. Nor did those Russians who looked for enlightenment to the west necessarily accept existing western institutions. Herzen, a professed westerner and democrat, had little use for the democratic institutions which he found at work in western Europe; and the Russian Marxists, who must be classified as westerners, none the less denounced the bourgeois democracy of the west.

On the other hand, the first Slavophils, scarcely less than the westerners, were in revolt against the repressive officialdom of Nicholas I. It is true that they purported to seek their ideal in an imaginary Russian past. But Slavophilism (which Pisarev called " a psychological phenomenon due to unsatisfied needs ") had even less to do with the facts

94

Some Nineteenth-Century Russian Thinkers

of that past than had the ideal of the westerners with the existing facts in western Europe. The original Slavophils were not champions of the Romanov autocracy; nor, when they spoke of Russia's mission to Europe, were they thinking in terms of political power. It was only in the second Slavophil generation of the eighteen-seventies, marked by Danilevsky's *Russia and Europe* and the later political essays of Dostoevsky, that Slavophilism degenerated into a crude form of Russian nationalism and provoked the challenge of the philosopher Soloviev: "What East do you want to be, the East of Xerxes or the East of Christ?"

Nor did the dichotomy of east and west wholly coincide with the other vital issues which tormented Russian nineteenth-century thinkers. In the grand debate between society and the individual, between authority and freedom, between the "eternal harmony" and the sacrifice of the innocent, which was pursued in one form or another throughout the great literature of the period, it would be misleading to assign the conflicting roles to the protagonists of east and west. It is true that westerners like Belinsky, Herzen and Mikhailovsky were particularly prone to assert the claims of the individual, and that Khomyakov the Slavophil imported into the debate the ecclesiastical word *Sobornost* (notoriously untranslatable, but meaning something rather more precise and more authoritative than "community-mindedness"). But it was Turgenev's nihilist Bazarov — a westerner if ever there was one — who maintained that it was as unscientific to study individual men

Studies in Revolution

and women as to study individual birch trees. The typical westerner Belinsky was as conscious of the underlying dilemma as the typical Slavophil (so far as concerns his later years) Dostoevsky and expresses it in strikingly similar terms.

Hegel opened the debate. His immense influence in Russia was beyond doubt due to the fact that he represented a reaction against the individualism of the Enlightenment, a victory, in Berdyaev's words, "of the general over the particular, of the universal over the individual, of society over personality". In the Russian argument over Hegel, Belinsky came to occupy the central place. He ran through the whole gamut of experience and changed his attitude to the extent of 180 degrees between the article on Griboedov, in which he exclaimed that "society is always juster and higher than the private person", and the letter to Botkin in which he declared that "the fate of the subject, of the individual, of the personality is more important than the fate of the whole world". The second position was that in which he ultimately found anchor. It was as a disciple of Belinsky that Ivan Karamazov was presently to say: "I renounce altogether the higher harmony; it is not worth the smallest tear of one tormented child".

Belinsky found his way out of the dilemma in the conception of a new society based on respect for the individual personality, on truth and justice — that is to say, in a socialism which was Utopian not so much in its organization as in its major premise. Dostoevsky sought his solution in a new synthesis

Some Nineteenth-Century Russian Thinkers

of freedom and authority through Orthodox Christianity: the Catholic synthesis he rejected as incompatible with freedom. But some critics have felt that Dostoevsky was more convinced of the logical necessity of his solution than of its cogency, and that he remained to the end a dual and divided personality. It will be readily conceded that Russian thinkers of the nineteenth century have plumbed these deep waters more profoundly than any of their predecessors; it will be less readily conceded that they have found firm ground on which their successors can build.

An outcrop of this controversy was the struggle to find a rational, utilitarian basis for morality and for art. Rationalism, said Khomyakov the Slavophil, was "the mortal sin of the west", and had infected Catholicism as much as other forms of western life. Dostoevsky's *Man from Underground* wanted to free humanity from the tyranny of two plus two equals four; and the Slavophil poet Tyutchev declared, in a couplet which remained famous, that it was impossible to comprehend Russia with the mind, it was possible only to believe in her. The conception that faith, and therefore morality, lay altogether beyond reason was rooted in Orthodox Christianity and in Russian thought.

The first westerners believed, by implication, in a rational morality. But it was Chernyshevsky who, substituting Feuerbach and Comte for Hegel as his masters in philosophy, imported into Russia the utilitarian philosophy of Bentham and Mill, whose *Principles of Political Economy* he translated into Russian.

Studies in Revolution

His enormously popular novel *What is to be Done?* depicted a set of young people actuated by what were supposed to be the purest principles of rational egoism — which, illogically enough, did not exclude the duty, eagerly recognized and accepted, of sacrificing one's immediate interest to those ultimate principles.

Pisarev, as usual, was responsible for the systematization and *reductio ad extremum* of the doctrine:

> The morality of men does not depend on their qualities of heart or nature, on abundance of virtue or absence of vice: words of this kind have no tangible meaning. The morality of this or that society depends exclusively on the question to what degree the members of the society are conscious of their own interests.

Moreover:

> In order to be a moral man it is indispensable to be to a certain degree a thinking man: but the faculty of thinking only becomes strong and well developed when the individual succeeds in escaping from the yoke of material necessity.

Here already are the solid foundations of class morality on which Engels was presently to build.

But more interest was excited by the controversy about art in which Pisarev was once more the protagonist. As Berdyaev points out, the west has never been conscious of a need to justify culture as such. The western world, including western Catholicism, has assimilated without question Greco-Roman culture and Greco-Roman humanism and combined it with the Christian tradition. The Orthodox Church, primarily eschatological in out-

98

Some Nineteenth-Century Russian Thinkers

look and severed from the traditions both of the Roman Empire and of the Renaissance, has always been implicitly hostile to the culture of this world. It was long before Russia acquired a secular literature or a secular art. In the nineteenth century two great writers, as far removed from each other in time and in point of view as Gogol and Tolstoy, both renounced and condemned their own artistic creation — a scarcely thinkable phenomenon in any western country.

Russian tradition was, then, less openly affronted than western tradition would have been when the young materialists of the 'sixties raised the question of the utility of art. Chernyshevsky, like Belinsky before him, frankly judged literary works by their content and was unconcerned with style. But his primary interest was not in literary criticism, and he formulated no very clear aesthetic theories. Dobrolyubov more boldly called literature " a subordinate force ", declaring that " its importance resides in propaganda, and its merit is determined by the content of this propaganda and the manner in which it is done ". Pisarev and a colleague named Zaitsev carried these views to their logical conclusion. Zaitsev, who seems to have anticipated Housman's discovery that artistic creation is accompanied by the physical symptom of a titillation of the spine, declared that " any artisan is more useful than any poet to the extent to which any positive number, however small, is greater than zero ". In an essay called *The Annihilation of Aesthetics*, which appeared in 1865, Pisarev described a famous

Studies in Revolution

Petersburg chef as a more useful member of society than Raphael, and added that he himself would rather be a Russian cobbler than a Russian Raphael.

Stated in this extreme form, such views ended by refuting themselves. But it would be rash to pretend that the utilitarian view of art was ever seriously supplanted by the opposition which Pisarev's challenge excited. The glorification of Pushkin by the Slavophils was an answer to Pisarev. But it was an answer on his own ground. Pushkin was not, as Pisarev had pretended, useless to society: on the contrary, he was highly valuable to it because he inculcated and encouraged a right view of man's place in it. Neither side denied that content was what ultimately mattered, or had any truck with anything that smacked of art for art's sake; not until the symbolist movement appeared at the turn of the century was this view seriously contested. Nor did anything happen to shake the conviction of the 'sixties that art was an essentially aristocratic and conservative phenomenon, while science was democratic and progressive. Such prejudices died hard in nineteenth-century Russia. It is not certain that they are dead to-day.

It remains to consider Russian nineteenth-century thought in its relation to the State. Berdyaev is hardly correct in claiming anarchism as " the creation of Russians ". The genealogy of anarchism goes back to William Godwin, if not farther: it was firmly embedded in the incipient socialist movements of western Europe before it established itself in Russia. But the significant point is that a

Some Nineteenth-Century Russian Thinkers

doctrine, which in western Europe was specifically socialist and revolutionary, coloured in Russia the thinking of the whole intelligentsia of whatever political complexion.

Political thought in nineteenth-century Russia, whether of westerners or of Slavophils, began in opposition to the bureaucratic State of Nicholas I. The first westerners, such as Herzen, were at best grudging advocates of the western democratic State; from the first, as Berdyaev says, the Russian idea of freedom was bound up, not with liberalism but with anarchism. The first Slavophils unreservedly treated the State — any State — as an evil. Dostoevsky passed, in his later years, for a fervent upholder of the autocracy. Yet the " Legend of the Grand Inquisitor ", though ostensibly directed against the secular arm of Catholicism, is in fact valid against any attempt to set up a " kingdom of this world ". Tolstoy, in theory, rejected not only the State but every exercise of power.

The struggle between Marx and Bakunin thus acquires fresh significance as a struggle between western and eastern conceptions of revolution, between the Jacobin conception of revolution through the State by seizing and using State power and the anarchist conception of revolution through the people by destroying the power of the State. Marx, it is true, paid tribute to socialist freedom by postulating the eventual dying away of the State. But his immediate concern was with the dictatorship of the proletariat. The essence of Bakunin's case

Studies in Revolution

against Marx was that Marx was a believer in State power — which the Russian anarchist regarded as a characteristically German trait.

When Lenin, steeped as he was in Russian as well as in Marxist thought, came to expound his view of the State in *State and Revolution*, at the critical moment of 1917, what he did was to refurbish the old western socialist tradition of hostility to the State, which remained embedded and half buried in classical Marxism, in order to convict the German Social-Democrats of a State worship incompatible with the fundamental tenets of Marx. Beelzebub was invoked to cast out Beelzebub. *State and Revolution*, with its double insistence on the immediate dictatorship of the proletariat and ultimate dying away of the State, is a characteristic synthesis of west and east, of Jacobinism and anarchism. It is a striking example of Lenin's superlative skill in rooting western revolutionary doctrines in congenial Russian soil.

Masaryk, the western liberal, who completed his survey of Russian thought before the revolution at a time when many western observers still believed in the prospect of a liberal and democratic evolution of Russian society, regarded the choice before Russia as one between theocracy and democracy. Berdyaev, the Orthodox philosopher, has a double advantage of standpoint. He writes as a Russian who understands — as no western liberal, however acute his perceptions, could ever understand — the lack of any foundation in Russian thought and tradition which could have carried the elaborate

Some Nineteenth-Century Russian Thinkers

and delicate structure of liberal democracy; and he writes after a revolution which, while it has provided no final synthesis for the contradictions of Russian nineteenth-century thought, has carried the debate a stage farther and, so to speak, shifted it on to another plane.

Whatever else may have changed, the fundamental theme of east and west has not ceased to play its customary part in the Russian politics and Russian thought of the last thirty years. Bolshevism is primarily a creation of western thought and experience. But the eastern element in it, and the growth of that influence in recent years, will not be seriously contested. It is possible to read the whole story of the defeat of Trotsky and the " old Bolsheviks ", who had spent their formative years in Europe and whose revolutionary outlook was predominantly western, by Stalin and a group whose background and training were mainly Russian and non-European, as a re-emergence in Russian history of the eastern factor temporarily eclipsed by its western counterpart.

Indeed, no understanding is possible of many of the outstanding characteristics of the Soviet regime without some study of the background of nineteenth-century Russia. The combination of a rigidly materialist outlook with a call, widely and fervently accepted, for self-sacrifice in the revolutionary cause; the demand for the liberation of human beings from exploitation through the pursuit of collective good, which in its turn threatens to become a new source of oppression; the demand for

Studies in Revolution

a philosophy which embraces politics, society and art and uses them as the expression of its purpose — all these are the direct legacy to Bolshevism of Russian radical thinkers of the nineteenth century.

The debt to the Slavophils, though in some respects paradoxical, is unmistakable. The rejection of bourgeois democracy, of bourgeois individualism, of bourgeois notions of property (Berdyaev himself remarks that "the Soviet constitution of 1936 enacted the best legislation in the world about property ") links Soviet theory and practice with a long line of Russian thinkers. The Russian messianism of the Slavophils, philosophical rather than political in its origin but susceptible of political perversions, reappears in the form of a messianism of the proletariat. "Communism", writes Berdyaev, "is a Russian phenomenon in spite of its Marxist ideology. Communism is Russian destiny; it is a moment in the inner destiny of the Russian people." This is an exaggeration of the specifically Russian aspects of Bolshevism, which may be dangerous if it induces the belief that Communism has no more than an external and episodic interest for other nations. But no student of Russian history will be tempted to ignore the grain of truth which it contains.

7

PLEKHANOV: FATHER OF RUSSIAN MARXISM

JUST thirty years after George Plekhanov's death, which occurred in Finland on June 12, 1918, an English translation of his principal philosophical essay has appeared under the title *In Defence of Materialism.*[1] Plekhanov was a prolific writer. But the twenty-four volume edition of his works, published in Moscow in the nineteen-twenties, is no longer easy to come by; and only a few of his essays and articles had hitherto been available in English. The present translation has been entrusted to the safe hands of Mr. Andrew Rothstein. It is preceded by an introductory sketch which is as accurate and masterly an account as could be desired of Plekhanov's career and significance.

The text-book label for Plekhanov is " the father of Russian Marxism ". In the words of one enthusiast, he " brought down the ten commandments of Marx from Sinai and delivered them to the youth of Russia ". He was Lenin's acknowledged teacher in

[1] G. V. Plekhanov, *In Defence of Materialism.* The Development of the Monist View of History. Translated by Andrew Rothstein. Lawrence and Wishart. 18s.

105

Studies in Revolution

Marxism, and laid the foundations of Russian Social-Democracy. Born in 1856, he graduated as a revolutionary in the Narodnik movement, breaking with it in 1880 on the issue of individual terrorism, which he rejected as futile and irrelevant. The assassination of Alexander II in 1881 led to a general round-up of revolutionaries; and Plekhanov was already abroad.

The next two years were decisive. The break with the Narodniks on the policy of terrorism, and the manifest bankruptcy of that policy after 1881, led Plekhanov to re-examine the basic tenets of the Narodnik philosophy — the belief that the peasantry was the coming revolutionary force in Russia. This belief, attested by a long tradition of peasant revolts and revolutionary peasant leaders, from Stenka Razin to Pugachev, was universally held in the west as in the east. Marx himself had encouraged the favourite Narodnik speculation that the Russian peasant commune was destined to evolve into a socialist society without an intervening capitalist stage.

Plekhanov's claim to an outstanding place among the makers of the October revolution is the insight, brilliantly original in the early eighteen-eighties, that capitalism was already in the process of striking roots in Russia, that its development would create a Russian proletariat, and that it was this Russian proletariat, and not the Russian peasantry, which would provide the driving-force and the ideological justification of the Russian revolution. There was thus no reason to place Russia outside the orthodox Marxist scheme. The trend of Plekhanov's thinking was apparent in 1882 when he published a Russian

Plekhanov: Father of Russian Marxism

translation of the *Communist Manifesto*, though the preface shows that he was not yet a Marxist. In the following year, with two of his close associates in exile, Paul Axelrod and Vera Zasulich, he founded a group under the name "The Liberation of Labour" with a Marxist programme. Plekhanov was the undisputed ancestor of Russian Social-Democracy, both as a doctrine and as an organization.

The ten years that followed were occupied by incessant controversy with the Narodniks. Plekhanov's position was defined in two essays dating from 1883 and 1884 respectively, *Socialism and the Political Struggle* and *Our Differences*; and the broad lines of policy here laid down were not seriously amended or added to for twenty years. Plekhanov asserted that the Russian peasantry was fundamentally non-revolutionary; that the peasant commune could evolve only into petty bourgeois capitalism, not into socialism; that the revolution would culminate in the seizure of power by the industrial workers; but that this final step could be taken only under conditions of bourgeois democracy, the achievement of which was therefore the first and immediate revolutionary goal. To count on a peasant revolt as the source of revolution was tantamount to anarchism; to advocate an immediate seizure of power by the workers was " Blanquism ". But these ideas made such slow headway that, when Plekhanov appeared in Paris in 1889 at the founding congress of the Second International and announced that " the Russian revolution will triumph as a proletarian revolution, or it will not triumph

Studies in Revolution

at all ", he was uttering a bold paradox.

Such was the picture when Lenin entered the lists with a vigorous polemic against the Narodniks in 1894. By this time Russian capitalism, under the powerful impulse of Witte, was growing by leaps and bounds; the first serious strikes and demonstrations of workers had occurred in Petrograd; and the views of Plekhanov were coming into their own. Small Marxist groups sprang up in the principal Russian cities. On the other hand, the authorities still saw revolution in terms of Narodniks and terrorists; and they were not displeased with the appearance of this new sect which was splitting the revolutionary movement, which did not appear to be preaching immediate action and which was mainly occupied in analysing the growth of Russian capitalism. For a few years the writings of the Marxists, provided they were couched in learned and not openly provocative language, received the *imprimatur* of the censors. It was the period of what came to be known as " legal Marxism ".

This curious circumstance explains why Plekhanov's chief philosophical work was also the only one of his writings legally published in Russia before the revolution. He completed it in London in 1894. It was copied out by an enthusiastic young Russian Marxist named Potresov, who carried the manuscript back with him to Petrograd and secured a publisher for it. The conditions of its publication also explain why the title originally chosen for it by Plekhanov (which has been restored in the present translation) was abandoned in favour of the meaning-

Plekhanov: Father of Russian Marxism

less and therefore harmless circumlocution, *On the Question of the Development of the Monist View of History.* It appeared in the last days of 1894, bearing the date 1895, and was at once read by Lenin, who expounded it with enthusiastic approval to the Marxist circle in Petrograd. It had an immediate and lasting success. Lenin afterwards said that it had " reared a whole generation of Russian Marxists ".

In Defence of Materialism (followed a year later by *Essays in the History of Materialism,* of which an English version is available) is a systematic, orderly and effective presentation in an historical setting of the Marxist doctrine of dialectical materialism. Starting from French eighteenth-century material-ism, which he traces back to Locke, Plekhanov then illustrates how the idea of the class struggle passed into French thought in the half-century after 1789, turns from this to the Utopian socialists and to German idealist philosophy, and finally shows how the " modern materialism " of Marx springs from all these diverse sources. Apart from some unduly lengthy polemics against contemporary Russian " subjectivists ", all this wears remarkably well. There is no better exposition available of what Marx (and Lenin) meant by dialectical materialism.

The essence of dialectical, as opposed to " meta-physical ", or static, materialism is to introduce the element of opposition, struggle and movement into the explanation of reality. This relieves materialism of the determinism implicit in the more rigid forms of the doctrine, but puts a question mark against the nature of the forces generating the dialectical

Studies in Revolution

process. In postulating that the ultimate source is to be found in changes in material conditions of production, Marx does not pretend that these operate automatically or without the conscious intervention of free human will. In a famous letter written in the last years of his life, Engels goes so far as to admit that he and Marx may sometimes have overstated the role of the " economic factor " and neglected the " other factors in the reciprocal interactions of the historical process". The doctrine of dialectical materialism thus gains in subtlety what it loses in the false simplicity sometimes attributed to it.

Translated (as all Marxist philosophy must be) into concrete political terms, the Marxist doctrine of man and matter raises the issue of the respective roles in revolutionary policy of the " spontaneous " action of the masses, which is dependent on objective material situations, and of " conscious " leadership, which is based on a study and grasp of revolutionary theory. The balance is so nice that writers and actors in the revolutionary drama are in constant danger of tipping it over on one side or the other. Plekhanov, while stating the doctrine fairly enough, leans on the whole towards those who count on the ripening of objective conditions to produce spontaneous action as the main revolutionary force. " History is made by the masses ", he wrote in a famous passage. ". . . While we are preparing the leaders of the revolutionary army, the officers and non-commissioned officers of the revolutionary army, that army itself is being created by the irreversible march of social developments."

Plekhanov: Father of Russian Marxism

Lenin, on the other hand, sometimes — notably in his famous pamphlet of 1902, *What is to be Done?* — went rather uncomfortably far in preaching the need of conscious leadership working " from without " on the otherwise inert masses. This idea dictated Lenin's conception of the Russian Social-Democratic Party as a small highly disciplined group of professional revolutionaries. Only thus could the masses be made ripe for revolution : " There is no conscious activity of the workers without social democracy ". It was this attitude which exposed Lenin from time to time to charges of " Blanquism " and " Bakuninism ". According to present interpretations, Lenin's and Stalin's main contribution to the theory of dialectical materialism has been " to reveal the active role of consciousness."

This divergence was the basis of the rift, doctrinal and temperamental, which was presently to open between Plekhanov and Lenin. But for the moment all was well. When Lenin visited the older man in Geneva on his first journey abroad in the summer of 1895 the relations were still those of revered master and brilliant disciple. On Lenin's return to Russia he was arrested in December 1895, and spent the next four years in prison or in Siberia. He was, however, able to follow and applaud Plekhanov's vigorous polemics against the " legal Marxists " and the " economists ", who were trying to empty Marxism of its revolutionary content by treating it as a pure theory of economic evolution; and he hailed with enthusiasm the first attempt in 1898 to create a Russian Social-Democratic Party.

Studies in Revolution

When Lenin emerged from exile in 1900 he met Potresov and another young revolutionary called Martov, and between them the three hatched a project to found a popular revolutionary journal and a solid Marxist periodical, to be called *Iskra* (" The Spark ") and *Zarya* (" The Dawn ") respectively, and to be issued somewhere in Europe. It was Potresov who, having well-to-do relations, furnished the funds and seems at the outset to have been the moving spirit in the enterprise. Mr. Rothstein, who oddly refers to Potresov as Plekhanov's " publisher ", ignores altogether Potresov's role in the foundation of *Iskra*, which he ascribes to Lenin alone. It is true that Potresov became a Menshevik in 1903, a " defencist " in 1914 and a bitter enemy of the Bolshevik revolution after 1917. But these subsequent falls from grace need not depose him from his distinguished niche in the pre-history of the revolution. Be this as it may, the three young men proceeded, one by one, to Switzerland to lay the scheme before Plekhanov and his group. Not without difficulty, agreement was reached. The journals were to be published with an editorial board consisting of Plekhanov, Axelrod and Zasulich, Lenin, Potresov and Martov.

The possibilities of friction were soon apparent. Plekhanov, the senior member and undisputed doyen of the group, remained in his own eyes and in those of others the presiding genius of the enterprise. Lenin quickly emerged head and shoulders above his fellow editors by his energy, by the clarity of his ideas, and by his determination to establish both a body of

Plekhanov: Father of Russian Marxism

revolutionary doctrine and an organized revolutionary party. The first of these aims required, in addition to filling the columns of *Iskra*, the promulgation of a party programme; the second, the summoning of a party congress to take up the work begun and abandoned in 1898.

Plekhanov sympathized with both these aims. He drafted a programme on the lines of those prepared fifteen and twenty years ago for the "Liberation of Labour" group. This was criticized by Lenin, and out of the subsequent discussions came the draft programme which was published in *Iskra* in the summer of 1902. Plekhanov's prestige was still great; and almost for the last time in his life Lenin was prepared to bow to superior authority, or at any rate to compromise with it. A significant "concession" secured by Lenin in these discussions was the inclusion in the programme of the Marxist doctrine of the "dictatorship of the proletariat", which had characteristically found no place in Plekhanov's draft. One of the charges brought by Lenin against Plekhanov many years later was his failure to deal with the relation of the revolution to the State.

The party congress, which met in Brussels and then in London in the summer of 1903, was more troublesome. It adopted the programme without difficulty, but split on the party rules. Here Lenin proposed a formula for party membership designed to cover his conception of the party as a disciplined army of trained and active revolutionaries. The prestige of the master had hitherto weighed with

Studies in Revolution

the disciple; but now the determination and force-fulness of the disciple carried away the master himself. Plekhanov supported Lenin throughout the congress. This did not save Lenin from being defeated on the issue of the rules. But by a turn of the wheel, his group secured a majority in the elections of party officers. This victory had two results. Lenin and his supporters are known to posterity as " Bolsheviks " or majority-men, leaving the title of " Mensheviks " to the minority; and Lenin and Plekhanov were left in undisputed control of *Iskra*, the organ of party policy.

Plekhanov had now reached the summit and turning-point of his career. Many explanations might be suggested of the next phase. Though he was not yet fifty, complaints about his health began to be heard at this time; he may have lacked the physical strength and endurance to cope with the younger rival who was driving him where he did not want to go. Plekhanov was by character a mild man — a man of the pen rather than of action. In words he could be trenchant enough. At the congress he had shocked the delegates, and provoked some hisses, by proclaiming, with a logic less faulty (unless the reporters have traduced him) than his Latin: *salus revolutiae suprema lex*. But in practice the cloak and dagger were antipathetic to him. Nature had fitted him to theorize about revolution, not to make it. Stalin rather unkindly lumps him with Kautsky among the " theorists " whose role is finished as soon as revolution actually begins.

Another cause of the split was diagnosed by

Plekhanov: Father of Russian Marxism

Krupskaya when she remarked that "after the turn of the century Plekhanov had lost the capacity for understanding Russia". Like all the early revolutionaries he had always been a "westerner" in terms of Russian nineteenth-century thought; and by 1901 he had lived continuously in western Europe for twenty years. He had imbibed the softer, as well as some of the more arid, traits of western rationalism and western radicalism — its humanitarianism, its belief in ordered progress, its dislike of violence and of abrupt or catastrophic change. He had incapacitated himself to understand the Russian revolution — or to understand Lenin.

In essence the rift between Plekhanov and Lenin was the same which divided Mensheviks from Bolsheviks. Both accepted the ordered sequence laid down in the *Communist Manifesto* according to which bourgeois democratic revolution was to be followed by proletarian socialist revolution. Both agreed that Russia was as yet only on the threshold of the bourgeois revolution, whose advent was being inevitably hastened by the development of Russian capitalism. Plekhanov, the theorist, in common with the Mensheviks, remained content with this tidy scheme. Lenin, the practical revolutionary, became from 1901 onwards increasingly impatient of a policy which, until some undefined date in the future, left the proletariat with little to hope for and little to do — except, perhaps, to further the progress of capitalism, its own greatest enemy and oppressor. It was when Lenin tried to escape from this dilemma, to hasten the bourgeois revolution by an alliance

Studies in Revolution

between the proletariat and the peasantry and to carry it forward at the earliest moment to the socialist stage, that he encountered the stern opposition, in the name of Marxist orthodoxy, of Plekhanov and the Mensheviks.

Psychologically and politically the break was overdue when Plekhanov and Lenin celebrated their joint victory at the 1903 congress. Plekhanov was quickly shocked by the ruthless consistency with which Lenin proposed to exploit the victory. The Mensheviks, whom Lenin wished to excommunicate, included most of Plekhanov's old friends and associates. The rigid party discipline in matters of opinion as well as of organization which Lenin wished to enforce was alien to Plekhanov's western notions of political organization and agitation. Unthinkably for Lenin, Plekhanov began to advocate reconciliation with the dissidents. Before the end of 1903 Lenin had resigned from the editorial board of *Iskra*; Plekhanov had co-opted on to it the former members rejected by the congress, Mensheviks all; *Iskra* had become a Menshevik organ; and Lenin had been left to organize his Bolsheviks as an independent faction.

The next twelve months saw a series of scathing articles from Plekhanov's pen against Lenin and the Bolsheviks. Lenin's *What is to be Done?* was answered by Plekhanov's *What not to Do*. Lenin was declared guilty of fostering a " sectarian spirit of exclusion ", of claiming to act " in obedience to an infallible class instinct ", of " confusing the dictatorship of the proletariat with the dictatorship

Plekhanov: Father of Russian Marxism

over the proletariat". Plekhanov was a learned controversialist. With a wealth of quotation he proved that Lenin, by his insistence on "consciousness", was reviving the idealistic heresy of the Bauer brothers which Marx had denounced in the eighteenforties, and that, by his advocacy of an army of professional revolutionaries, he was a disciple not of Marx but of Bakunin. It is perhaps significant (though there was provocation for this on the other side) that Plekhanov's arguments turn always on the issue of conformity with Marx, never on that of the practical utility of the courses of action proposed. Plekhanov remained to the end doctrinaire and academic.

The rest of his career was one of wavering and frustration. He never became an orthodox Menshevik, and in the party controversies of the following years occasionally even found himself in Lenin's camp. The last meeting between the two men happened after the outbreak of war in 1914. Plekhanov, ten years earlier, at the time of the Russo-Japanese war, had ardently preached "defeatism" and the class war, and had written that "international social-democracy cannot help rising in revolt against international wars". He now appeared as an advocate of national defence on a Socialist platform at Lausanne, and found himself suddenly and unexpectedly confronted by an angry Lenin. Krupskaya, who relates the incident, admits that a majority of the audience was on the side of Plekhanov.

In the spring of 1917 the February revolution

Studies in Revolution

allowed Plekhanov to return to Russia after an interval of thirty-six years. He took part in the famous " democratic conference " in Moscow in August, and denounced the Bolsheviks both before and after the October revolution. For a reissue of his thirty-four-year-old essay on *Socialism and the Political Struggle* he wrote a postscript (it has not been reprinted in the collected edition), in which he accused Lenin of reviving an old Narodnik heresy by supposing that the introduction of socialism could be made to coincide with the overthrow of the old regime, and predicted " fearful harm " from the attempt to telescope the bourgeois and proletariat revolutions. When over-zealous Red Guards ransacked the house in Tsarskoe Selo where Plekhanov lay sick, his friends protested to Lenin ; and an order was issued in the name of the Council of People's Commissars " to protect the person and property of citizen Plekhanov ". The material guarantee was thus accompanied by a verbal insult. Plekhanov was no longer a socialist " comrade " but a bourgeois " citizen ".

Plekhanov was now in an advanced stage of tuberculosis, and died before the revolution was a year old. At his own request he was buried in Petrograd near the grave of Belinsky. The request was significant of Plekhanov's political affinities in his later years. Belinsky — the typical " man of the 'forties " — had evolved from the position of a Hegelian conservative to that of a Hegelian political radical. He ended where Marx began, and, dying young, was always in the vanguard of his own con-

Plekhanov: Father of Russian Marxism

temporaries. Plekhanov's main work of providing a Marxist foundation for the revolutionary cause of Russia was done by the time he was forty; and though he lived on to recede to a position not far from that where Belinsky had ended, his achievement gives him a lasting place among Russian thinkers. He is perhaps the only man who, having crossed swords with Lenin in bitter controversy, is to-day quoted with respect in the Soviet Union.

8

THE CRADLE OF BOLSHEVISM

WHAT became the "All-Russian (afterwards All-Union) Communist Party (Bolsheviks)" was founded at Minsk fifty years ago, under the name of the "Russian Social-Democratic Workers' Party", by a tiny congress of nine men. They represented local organizations at Petersburg, Moscow, Kiev and Ekaterinoslav, and the "Jewish General Workers' Union in Russia and Poland", commonly called the "Bund". The congress lasted three days — March 13-15 (March 1-3, O.S.), 1898. It authorized the publication of a manifesto (which was drafted by Peter Struve, a Marxist intellectual), appointed a central committee and decided to issue a party organ. But before anything else could be done, the police arrested all the principal participants, so that virtually nothing remained of this initial effort save a common name shared by a number of local committees and organizations which had no central rallying point and no other connexions with one another.

The manifesto, after referring to the " life-giving hurricane of the 1848 revolution ", which had blown over Europe fifty years before, noted that the

The Cradle of Bolshevism

Russian working-class was "entirely deprived of what its foreign comrades freely and peacefully enjoy — a share in the administration of the State, freedom of the spoken and written word, freedom of organization and assembly". These were necessary instruments in the struggle "for its final liberation, against private property, for socialism". In the west the bourgeoisie had won these freedoms. In Russia conditions were different.

The farther east one goes in Europe, the weaker, meaner and more cowardly becomes the bourgeoisie in the political sense, and the greater the cultural and political tasks which fall to the lot of the proletariat. On its strong shoulders the Russian working class must and will carry the work of conquering political liberty. This is an essential step, but only the first step, to the realization of the great historic mission of the proletariat, to the foundation of a social order in which there will be no place for the exploitation of man by man.

In western democratic terms, the programme was extreme but constitutional. In Tsarist Russia it was unconditionally revolutionary; the intention to "throw off the yoke of the autocracy" was specifically proclaimed.

Nearly three years later a fresh start was made when the three young revolutionary Marxists — Lenin, Potresov and Martov — who had just served sentences in Siberia for illegal activities met the "Liberation of Labour" group in Switzerland. Lenin was then thirty. Since 1894, when his first political writing had been circulated in hectograph form, he had been known as an able and

Studies in Revolution

vigorous disciple of Plekhanov; and he had been, before his arrest in December 1895, a leading spirit in one of the groups represented at the 1898 congress. He now showed himself the most energetic member of the *Iskra* board. It was he who drafted the manifesto announcing the new journal, and who was its steadiest and most prolific contributor. It was he who led the agitation for a second party congress to take up again the work begun and interrupted at Minsk. The congress, which opened in July 1903, was the real founding congress of the party — not the less because its concluding stage also produced the epoch-making split between Bolsheviks and Mensheviks. The breach was intensified when, three months after the congress, the wavering Plekhanov went over to the Mensheviks, Lenin resigned from the board and *Iskra* became a Menshevik organ.

The party thus founded in 1898, refounded in 1903 and (so far as its Bolshevik wing was concerned) remodelled by Lenin after the split, became the directing instrument of the revolution of October 1917. The congress of 1903 was the crucial turning-point in its history, the focus round which all the main party controversies, both earlier and later, revolved. Some understanding of these controversies is essential to any judgment on the revolution itself and on the events which issued from it. The English reader can find an account of them in the unsatisfactory official short *History of the Communist Party of the Soviet Union*, published in 1938, or in Popov's less cursory *Outline History of the Communist*

The Cradle of Bolshevism

Party of the Soviet Union, published five years earlier. The Russian reader is embarrassed only by the mass of often indigestible and unreliable material. An important recent accession to the Russian sources of party history is *The Origin of Bolshevism,* by F. I. Dan,[1] the former Menshevik leader, who died almost at the moment of its publication in New York. The last chapter contains what is virtually a recantation of Dan's previous attitude, and the book represents a sincere, though not uncritical, acceptance of Lenin's views. It bears some of the marks of a work of old age, but is full both of knowledge and of penetration. No more objective account of early party history has been written by any of those who participated in it.

When the 1903 congress met, three ideological battles had been fought and won; and these three victories formed the basis of the party programme unanimously adopted by the congress. As against the Narodniks, the Russian Social-Democratic Workers' Party regarded the proletariat and not the peasant as the bearer of the coming revolution; as against the "legal Marxists", it preached revolutionary action and no compromise with the bourgeoisie; as against the "economists", it emphasized the essentially political character of the party programme.

The campaign against the Narodniks had been conducted by Plekhanov in the 'eighties and early 'nineties. "The Russian revolution", ran Plekhanov's famous aphorism, "will triumph as

[1] F. I. Dan, *Proiskhozhdenie Bolshevizma.*

Studies in Revolution

a proletarian revolution, or it will not triumph at all." This clearly meant that the way to revolution in Russia would be paved by industrial development; and in the last decade of the century Witte and foreign capitalists were busy fulfilling this requirement. Lenin, in the writings against the Narodniks which opened his polemical career, had little to do but to drive home Plekhanov's arguments and to point tellingly to what was happening in Russia before the eyes of all. The star of the industrial worker was rising, the star of the backward peasant waning, in the revolutionary firmament. It was not until 1905 that the problem of fitting the Russian peasant into the revolutionary scheme again became a burning party issue.

The struggle against the "legal Marxists", whose views, expressed in slightly cryptic language, were allowed by the censorship to appear in learned journals, was more complicated. The ablest member of the group was Peter Struve, author of the manifesto of the Minsk congress; and Bulgakov and Berdyaev, who later joined the Orthodox Church, were at one time members of it. Lenin welcomed the temporary alliance of the "legal Marxists" against the Narodniks. They accepted without qualification the Marxist view of the development of capitalism as a first step towards the eventual achievement of socialism, and believed that in this respect Russia must tread the western path. So far Lenin agreed with them. But insistence on the necessity of the capitalist stage led them to treat this development as an end in itself and to substitute

The Cradle of Bolshevism

reform for revolution as the process out of which socialism would eventually grow; and it was on this point that Lenin attacked " legal Marxism " as tantamount to democratic liberalism and the enemy of the proletariat.

This attitude towards the " legal Marxists " was symptomatic of a dilemma which pursued the party for many years. Marxist theory from the *Communist Manifesto* onwards made it clear that, so long as political freedom had not been achieved, the proletariat shared with the bourgeoisie the same interest in winning it. In pursuance of this theory the party programme adopted by the second congress laid it down that the party " supports every opposition and revolutionary movement directed against the existing social and political order in Russia ". It was a rather undistinguished delegate to the congress who pointed out that only two contemporary movements answered to this description — the Social-Revolutionaries (who were the heirs of the Narodniks) and the " legal Marxists " — and that the congress had passed resolutions specifically condemning both of them. No ready reply was forthcoming. Whatever Marxist theory required, co-operation between the proletariat and the bourgeoisie for a specific end, common to both, could never be free from embarrassment so long as the destruction of the bourgeoisie remained the ultimate goal of the proletarian revolution. This inherent contradiction, and not the intolerance of Lenin or his successors, was responsible for a long-standing crux.

The " economists ", against whom the third

Studies in Revolution

ideological battle of these years was fought, were a group of Marxist intellectuals who in the autumn of 1897 started in Petersburg a journal called *The Workers' Thought*. Like the "legal Marxists", they remained within the constitutional framework, eschewed revolution and treated socialism as a distant ideal. Unlike the "legal Marxists", who confined themselves to theory, they had a programme of action. The advance to socialism must be by stages. At the present stage in Russia, the class-consciousness of the worker could be stimulated by encouraging him to concentrate on economic demands for economic ends, to better his condition by trade-union organization, mutual aid, self-education and so forth.

Meanwhile, political action must be reserved for the intellectuals; and, since there was as yet no basis for a Marxist political programme, that action could only take the form of supporting the liberal bourgeoisie in their demand for political freedom. In the words of the document which served as the manifesto of the group:

Discussions about an independent workers' political party are nothing but the result of transferring foreign problems and foreign solutions to our soil. . . . For the Russian Marxist there is one way out: to help the economic struggle of the proletariat and to participate in the activity of the liberal opposition.

In other words, the immediate objective in Russia could only be to reach the position long ago established in the west by the bourgeois revolution.

"Economism" received a forceful impulse from the

The Cradle of Bolshevism

wave of industrial strikes which began to sweep over Russia in 1896, and it was for five years an influential movement, perhaps the most influential movement, among Russian Marxists. But it was at once denounced by Plekhanov in Switzerland and by Lenin and his fellow-exiles in Siberia as a denial of the essence of Social-Democracy. The controversy was carried on into the *Iskra* period; and a good part of Lenin's first major work, *What is to be Done?* published in 1902, was devoted to a polemic against the " economists ". Political as well as economic agitation was needed to arouse the class-consciousness of the masses.

The ideal of the Social-Democrat must be not a trade-union secretary, but *a tribune of the people.* . . . A trade-union policy for the working class is simply a *bourgeois policy* for the working class.

When the second party congress met in 1903, the three tendencies represented by the Narodniks, the " legal Marxists " and the " economists " appeared to have received their death-blow, being almost unanimously denounced by the delegates — by future Mensheviks as well as by future Bolsheviks. Yet it was a Pyrrhic victory. The Social-Revolutionaries took up the unanswered challenge of the Narodniks; and the Mensheviks came to occupy positions scarcely distinguishable from those of the " legal Marxists " and of the " economists ". Nor was this an accidental perversity. The issue of fitting the Russian peasant into the Marxist scheme of proletarian revolution had not yet been faced; and the tragic contradictions of the attempt to make a

127

Studies in Revolution

socialist revolution in a country where no bourgeois revolution had yet occurred to win political freedom, had not been resolved.

It was against the background of these controversies that Lenin built up the future " All-Union Communist Party (Bolsheviks) ". He accused the Mensheviks, as he had once accused the " economists ", of lack of principle; " opportunism " meant for Lenin not a shifting of ground for tactical reasons (this he admitted and advocated freely enough) but a postponement of revolutionary work on the pretext that conditions were not ripe. But most of all he accused them of lack of organization, of amateurishness, of " small-scale craftsmanship ". The most significant division at the second congress was not the critical vote or the elections but the division on the party statute. Was the party, like western political parties, to be a mass organization of supporters and sympathizers? Or was it to be a disciplined army of active revolutionaries?

The question of organization thus raised a vital question of principle. Everything that has been most controversial in the history of the Russian revolution was involved in it. In the Menshevik view, the socialist revolution could be achieved only as the sequel of a bourgeois revolution and through a political party of the kind which had emerged from the bourgeois revolutions of the west. In the Bolshevik view, the Russian socialist revolution must carry within itself the bourgeois revolution which the Russian bourgeoisie had failed to achieve;

The Cradle of Bolshevism

and this called for a special form of party organization unknown to the west. In a sense both were right. Lenin, with his unerring perception of realities, knew the only way in which the Russian revolution could be led to victory. But if the survivors of Menshevism were to-day to retort that this is not the socialist revolution as understood by them or by the world in the early 1900s it would be difficult to prove them wrong. History disappoints the programme-makers as often as it refutes the prophets.

It must then be confessed, if justice is to be done, that Lenin's conception of the party, which he drove home after 1903 with all the ruthlessness of extreme consistency and unshakable conviction, owed much less to theory than to his own intuition of Russian requirements. If he accused the " economists " of exaggerating the case for " spontaneity " in the workers' movement, and declared that the class-consciousness of the workers could be developed only " from without " by an organized party of revolutionary intellectuals, the argument, however theoretical and general in form, was a faithful record of particular observed facts of Russian society. Lenin's conception of the party had at least the empirical justification that it was the kind of party required to make the revolution triumph in Russia. His opponents were prescribing for conditions which did not exist.

Lenin had two essential prerequisites for a revolutionary party : it must be small in numbers and disciplined and conspiratorial in character.

Studies in Revolution

While Plekhanov and Lenin both preached that
" history is made by the masses ", both recognized
that the main business of the party was to train the
" officers and non-commissioned officers of the revolutionary army ". Social conditions would provide
the rank and file when the moment arrived. For
Lenin the party was always a minority and its
backbone would always be a group of professional
revolutionaries. The 1905 revolution for the first
time brought a significant number of workers into
the party; and from that time Lenin began, for
tactical reasons, to emphasize the importance of the
role of the workers in the party. But it was not until
some years after 1917 that workers began to form
more than a small minority of the delegates to party
congresses or of the members of party committees.

Lenin's second prerequisite for the party — its
disciplined and conspiratorial character — derived
even more directly from Russian conditions. Isolated revolutionary groups of workers and students
in Russia, well-meaning amateurs, quickly fell
victims to the police, as Lenin himself had done. In
order to maintain secret revolutionary groups and
conduct secret revolutionary propaganda in Russia
itself, organization and discipline were paramount.
While the principles of democracy were professed
within the party, the necessities of the case precluded,
as Lenin explicitly recognized, anything like public
and open discussion or the election of leaders. Russian
conditions dictated a form of organization utterly
alien to the political parties of the west.

The attempt to execute a western political

The Cradle of Bolshevism

programme — for such Marxism essentially was —
in the conditions of the autocratic police State of the
Romanovs created a series of contradictions which
were the tragic dilemma of the Communist Party
and of the Bolshevik revolution. It was impossible
to attain a congruence of means and ends where
the indispensable means belonged to a different
order of society from that in and for which the
ends had been conceived. It was impossible to
establish a stable or rational relation with the bourgeoisie, domestic or foreign, since the doctrine
appeared to impose two contradictory attitudes,
alliance being alternately sought and spurned.
Finally it was impossible to create in terms of men
and women that basis of democratic administration
on which socialism of the kind contemplated in the
Marxist tradition could alone rest.

All these dilemmas emerge clearly from the bitter
debates which accompanied the founding of the
party and its initial steps in organization forty and
fifty years ago. The party moved forward on the
course set by Lenin inexorably, in spite of every
set-back, through an ever-tightening discipline and
an ever-narrowing circle of authority and power.
In the 1890s it had already been established that
the proletariat must lead the revolution; the
dictatorship of the proletariat was naturalized in
Russia. In 1903 it became accepted doctrine that
the party must lead the proletariat; and the
"dictatorship of the party" was a phrase long in use.
Then came the phase of the leadership of the party
by its central committee; this was the period of the

Studies in Revolution

revolution itself. After the introduction of the New Economic Policy in 1921 Lenin himself tightened the reins once more; and for a time the Politbureau of the party was the decisive organ, taking precedence over all other party and State institutions. Finally, when the restraint of Lenin's personal prestige was withdrawn, leadership passed to an inner group whose composition was never certainly known and which had no constitutional standing even within the party. The process had been precisely foreseen by Trotsky (of all people — since none was more dictatorial than he by temperament and ambition), who in a brilliant pamphlet published in 1904 predicted a situation in which " the party is replaced by the organization of the party, the organization by the central committee, and finally the central committee by the dictator ".

It would be difficult to pretend that Lenin in these early years of the party's history saw clearly whither the demand for rigid organization and discipline would lead. It would be even more difficult to pretend that, had he seen, he would have recoiled from the choice. His mind and heart were set on the revolution, in which he saw the crowning necessity for Russia and for the world. He would reject or neglect nothing that could contribute to its consummation.

Yet the unresolved dilemma remains. Dan brilliantly diagnoses the " immanent contradiction " in Russia's social development: its " retarded character ", which had brought it to the point of revolution only when socialism was already knocking at

The Cradle of Bolshevism

the door and democracy could no longer be realized without socialism, and its " backwardness ", which prevented the " realization of socialism in free democratic forms ". The words come from Dan's concluding chapter, which is, in effect, a renunciation of his former Menshevism and an acceptance of Lenin's conclusions and policy. Precisely because he recognizes the tragedy and the contradictions which, however inescapable they may have been, lay behind that policy, Dan's book constitutes a more powerful apologia for the party and for the revolution than the stereotyped official histories.

9

LENIN: THE MASTER BUILDER

Few great men have so quickly won so secure and uncontested a place in history as Lenin. Even those who most hated Lenin's work have praised his comparative moderation and statesmanship as a foil to the blacker villainy, first of his colleagues, then of his successors. Death removed him at a moment when the clouds of contemporary calumny had begun to disperse and before he had time to become involved in the embittered controversies which generally attend the consolidation of a revolution. For his own generation he stood out head and shoulders from his contemporaries by the length and devotion of his service to the cause, by the clarity and forcefulness of his ideas, and by his practical leadership in the critical moments of 1917. For the next generation he became the embodiment of the victorious revolution, his writings its sacred text.

Lenin, for all his fame as a revolutionary leader, was a creator rather than a destroyer. He played no personal part in the events of 1905 or in the February revolution of 1917; nor were Bolshevik ideas an important contributory factor. What

Lenin: The Master Builder

Lenin achieved in October 1917 was not the overthrow of the provisional government — that followed logically from all that had gone before, and was bound to happen — but the construction of something to take its place. The decisive moment of the revolution came when, at the first congress of Soviets in June 1917, an orator remarked from the platform that there was no revolutionaiy party willing to take over the responsibilities of government, and Lenin, amid mocking laughter, retorted from his place in the hall, " There is such a party ". Only when the new regime had taken over did Lenin rise to his full stature as administrator, head of government, organizer and supreme political tactician.

Lenin was also a builder, or re-builder, of his country's international status and authority. The great Russian Empire, when the Bolsheviks took possession of it and for some time after, was in a process of rapid disintegration — the result of internal turmoil and of defeat in war. The Brest-Litovsk treaty of March 1918 lopped off not only those western appendages of the former Tsarist realm whose independence the Soviet Government had spontaneously recognized, but a large slice of predominantly Russian territory. The summer of 1918 saw the beginning of civil war and British, French, Japanese and American intervention, which long outlasted the German collapse, and for more than two years forcibly divided the country between several conflicting authorities. Meanwhile Bolshevik acceptance of the right of self-determination and secession for all nations and national groups

135

Studies in Revolution

appeared to favour the process of dispersal and to rule out anything like a reconstitution of former unity.

Yet by the end of 1922, little more than two years after the victorious conclusion of the civil war, the diverse units had been gathered into the fold of the newly established Union of Soviet Socialist Republics (the formal incorporation of the two Central Asian republics was delayed till 1924) ; and the cohesion of the new federation was destined to prove at least as strong and enduring as that of the defunct empire. This consummation, which few could have foreseen in the dark days of 1918 or 1920, was not the least remarkable of Lenin's achievements. In the eyes of history he appears not only as a great revolutionary, but as a great Russian.

Public interest in Lenin, in his own country and elsewhere, shows no signs of abating. The second and third editions of his complete works (really two issues in different format of the same edition) were published between 1926 and 1932. Shortly before the war a fourth edition was decided on, and its publication is now in progress. The copious additional material appearing in these volumes had for the most part been published in the *Leninskii Sbornik* or other periodical publications, so that it is not, strictly speaking, new; but its inclusion in a new edition of the works makes it, for the first time, conveniently accessible.

On the other hand, the lengthy and valuable expository notes and the appendices of documents (often convenient, even if the documents could be found elsewhere) have disappeared. An official

Lenin: The Master Builder

pronouncement of 1938 had already condemned "crude political errors of a damaging character in the appendices, notes and commentaries to some volumes of the works of Lenin"; and the Marx-Engels-Lenin Institute has evidently shrunk from the task of revising them in the light of more recent information and a more up-to-date orthodoxy. The new edition appears with a slender and quite inadequate apparatus of notes; for this purpose the student will still have to use the earlier editions.

Meanwhile English students of Lenin will be assisted by two new publications. A complete English translation of Lenin's works, started in the 'thirties, has apparently been abandoned. But *The Essentials of Lenin,* translated from a Russian two-volume edition of his principal works, includes some which have not before appeared in English.[1] The volumes are large, the price low; and, while there are omissions to be regretted (including all but a few of Lenin's speeches and reports to congresses), the main corpus of Lenin's writings is now easily access-ible to the English reader. The other new book is a short popular biography by Mr. Christopher Hill[2] which easily outdistances any of its predecessors except that of D. S. Mirsky, now nearly twenty years old.

Mr. Hill, whose mandate from the series in which the book appears is " to open up a significant theme

[1] *The Essentials of Lenin.* In two volumes. Lawrence and Wishart. 12s. 6d. each.
[2] Christopher Hill, *Lenin and the Russian Revolution.* Hodder and Stoughton. 5s.

Studies in Revolution

by way of a biography of a great man ", has obviously been cramped by limitations of space. Apart from the usual biographical details and a concluding chapter of appreciation, he has chosen to concentrate on a few essential topics — Lenin's conception of the party, his agrarian policy, his philosophy of the State, his view of the relations of the revolutionary republic with the outside world and his economic policy. The choice of topics is judicious, and the handling sensible and accurate. The non-specialist reader, for whom the book is designed, will obtain from it a very fair and readable presentation of the main problems Lenin had to face and of his methods of solving them.

The central focus of Lenin's thought and action was his theory of the State, which found its most mature expression in *State and Revolution*, written on the eve of the October revolution and published in the spring of 1918. The socialist tradition from Godwin onwards had been almost unreservedly hostile to the State. Marx, especially in his early works, repeatedly denounces the State — " the form of organization adopted by the bourgeoisie for the guarantee of its property and interests ". The *Communist Manifesto*, true to this tradition, looked forward to the day when, differences between classes having been wiped out, " social power will lose its political character ". But the *Manifesto* also concerned itself with the more immediate practical step of winning the revolution ; and for this purpose it was necessary that the proletariat should " establish its supremacy by

Lenin: The Master Builder

overthrowing the bourgeoisie " and the State become identical with " the proletariat organized as the ruling class ". This was the idea which Marx crystallized a few years later into the famous slogan of " the dictatorship of the proletariat ".

The doctrine of the State, as it emerged from the writings of Marx and Engels, was twofold. In the long run the State, being a product of class contradictions and an instrument of oppression, would die away and have no place in the communist order of the future. In the short run, the proletariat, having destroyed the bourgeois State instrument by revolution, would have to set up a temporary State instrument of its own — the dictatorship of the proletariat — until such time as the classless society had been achieved. The reconciliation of the two points of view was not always easy. Orthodoxy, when Lenin first began to consider the matter, had to steer a careful course between the Scylla of anarchism, which rejected the State so vehemently as to exclude also the dictatorship of the proletariat, and the Charybdis of State socialism, especially dangerous in Germany, where the Lassallean tradition encouraged the belief that socialism might triumph, not by destroying the bourgeois State, but by allying itself with the existing State power.

Lenin, when he wrote *State and Revolution*, was still smarting from the " treachery " of the German Social-Democrats in embracing the national cause in 1914, and was therefore more impressed by the dangers of State worship than by those of anarchism. This makes the work a little one-sided. The

Studies in Revolution

argument against the anarchists in defence of the dictatorship of the proletariat occupies only a few hurried paragraphs; the bulk of the pamphlet is an assault on those pseudo-Marxists who refuse to recognize, first, that the State is a product of class antagonisms and an instrument of class domination, doomed to disappear with the disappearance of the classes themselves, and secondly, that the immediate goal is not the taking over of the bourgeois State machine, but its destruction and the substitution of the dictatorship of the proletariat.

For the student of history the most important passages in *State and Revolution* are those which show how Lenin at this time conceived the dictatorship of the proletariat. It is "something which is no longer properly a State"; it is "already a transitional State, no longer a State in the proper sense". It will "begin to die away immediately after its victory". Marx and Engels believed themselves to have discovered the prototype of the dictatorship of the proletariat in the Paris commune of 1871; in April 1917 Lenin eagerly transferred the discovery to the Soviets. The point of the discovery was that neither the commune nor the Soviets were "a State in the proper sense". Both had the same exclusively working-class representation and the same basis of voluntary self-organization, and stood for the same kind of loose federation of like-minded autonomous units in place of the sovereign authority of the bourgeois State. Both were to exercise administrative as well as legislative functions, and the evils both of regular armies and of a regular bureaucracy

Lenin: The Master Builder

were to be superseded. A militia of workers was to displace the army. Most of the administration would be managed by the workers themselves in their spare time.

Under socialism [wrote Lenin] much of " primitive " democracy will inevitably revive, since for the first time in the history of civilized societies the *mass* of the population will be raised to independent participation not only in voting and elections, *but in day-to-day administration.* Under socialism *all* will administer in turn and will quickly become accustomed to nobody administering.

It is often said that these somewhat Utopian projects applied only to the coercive organs of administration, not to the economic and financial apparatus. But this is not altogether true. Lenin at first believed that the tasks of business management and accounting, like those of administration, could be carried out by ordinary citizens. He observed that these tasks have been " extraordinarily simplified " by capitalism and reduced " to uncommonly simple operations of checking and registration within the reach of every literate person, to a knowledge of the four rules of arithmetic and to the handing out of correct receipts ". What was wrong about these aspirations was in part, no doubt, an over-optimistic estimate of human nature, but most of all a failure to understand that the dictatorship of the proletariat, or any form of socialist society, would involve not a reduction, but an immense increase, both in the numbers of those engaged in administration and in the complexity of their work.

Studies in Revolution

In three years Lenin learned much. On the eve of the introduction of NEP in the spring of 1921 he dismissed as a " fairy tale " the idea that every worker could " know how to administer the State ". Harsh necessity forced the Soviet administration into the traditional State mould which Lenin had never intended for it. Yet, so long as Lenin lived, something remained of the large-minded distrust of the State which he had expressed in *State and Revolution*. The Soviets, and especially the local Soviets, retained a wide measure of autonomy and initiative, even if their competence did not stray far from the parish pump; and Lenin continued with his last official breath to preach the need for untiring vigilance in curbing and controlling bureaucracy. Not till many years after Lenin's death did the inexorable tide of events re-establish a degree of State worship which would have seemed unthinkable to the men who made the revolution.

Lenin's personal share in moulding the foreign policy of the new regime was even more important and decisive than in shaping its domestic policy; and here, too, the same flexibility, the same readiness to study and follow the dynamic of events, is equally conspicuous. The foreign policy of the young Soviet Government was made up of three distinct strands — of radical pacifism, of world revolution and of national or State interest. The three strands sprang from different origins and could rarely be isolated in practice : the subtle web into which they were deftly woven was mainly Lenin's own work.

The *motif* of radical pacifism was particularly

Lenin: The Master Builder

strong during the first weeks and months of the revolution for two reasons. In the first place the Bolshevists were still vitally dependent, in the Soviets and elsewhere, on the support of the peasants and of their Social-Revolutionary leaders. The peasant masses, including the mobilized masses, were wholly indifferent, after more than three years of war, either to the defence of national interests or to the spread of world revolution. Their unconditional demand for peace was reflected in the ideology of those radical democrats who proclaimed without qualification or analysis that peace was always in the interest of the people everywhere, and that to follow and carry out the will of the people was the sure way to peace. Secondly, this radical pacifism was the basis of the political thinking of Woodrow Wilson and of those Left-wing circles in other countries where alone the Soviet regime might still hope to find friends. It was thus essential to dwell on the one point of view which seemed to provide a bridge between the regime and these potential supporters rather than on those aspects of Soviet policy which would inevitably divide them.

Such was the principal inspiration of the famous " decree on peace " which was the first public act of Soviet foreign policy. Its language is not Marxist but Wilsonian. It must be interpreted, not as some remote descendant of the *Communist Manifesto*, but as the forerunner of the Fourteen Points issued just two months later. What is demanded is not a socialist but a " just, democratic " peace — a peace " without annexations or indemnities ", a peace

143

Studies in Revolution

based on the right of self-determination for all nations by " a free vote " The decree declares secret diplomacy abolished and announces the intention — which was promptly carried out — to publish the secret treaties of the past : future negotiations were to be conducted — and this too was carried out at Brest-Litovsk — " completely openly before the whole people ".

Nothing is said, in the decree, of capitalism as the cause of war or of socialism as its cure. The one hint of world revolution occurs in the final injunction to the workers of England, France and Germany to assist their Russian comrades " to bring to successful conclusion the work of peace and also the work of liberating the labouring and exploited masses of the population from every kind of slavery and exploitation " The decree reflects, above all, that radical belief in the rightness and efficacy of mass opinion which was so deeply rooted in nineteenth-century democratic doctrine — the appeal from wicked governments to enlightened people, which had been a commonplace of Wilson's utterances. This note was echoed much later, though with rapidly diminishing sincerity, in Soviet pronouncements about disarmament.

The second strand in Soviet foreign policy — the promotion of world revolution — did not, however, long remain in the background. Peace at any price, however deep the psychological roots of its appeal and however great its political expediency at this juncture, was difficult to reconcile with fundamental Bolshevik doctrine ; and the policy of transforming

144

Lenin: The Master Builder

the imperialist war in all belligerent countries into civil war for the overthrow of capitalism had been too assiduously proclaimed to be discarded overnight. During the first weeks of the revolution enormous importance was attached to the spread of propaganda in the German armies by fraternization and by the distribution of literature; and less successful attempts were made to set propaganda on foot in the allied countries. For a brief moment this mood was all-powerful and all-pervading. Trotsky, on the testimony of his autobiography, went to the Commissariat of Foreign Affairs believing that his task was to publish the secret treaties, "issue a few revolutionary proclamations" and then shut up shop. World revolution would take care of the rest. Foreign affairs in the accepted sense would cease to exist.

But the third strand in Soviet foreign policy — national interest — was not slow to assert itself. Lenin, with his sense of realism, was the first to perceive that a Soviet republic, living even for a limited period in a world of States, would be compelled in many respects to behave like any other State. In an article in 1915, which afterwards did manful service in the controversy about "socialism in one country", Lenin had pointed out that the country or countries in which socialism was first victorious would have to stand up for a time against an agglomeration of hostile capitalist States; and in 1917, when some stalwart internationalist put up the slogan "Down with frontiers", Lenin sensibly replied that the Soviet republic, coming into existence in a capitalist world, would necessarily have

Studies in Revolution

State frontiers, as well as other State interests, to defend. If the rest of the world was organized on a system of States, it was not open to a single region to contract out of the system by an act of will.

It would, however, be rash to deduce from all this either a theoretical or a practical clash in Soviet foreign policy between the claims of world revolution and those of national interest. It was this clash, and the priority given to national interest, which had in Lenin's view destroyed the Second International. No such clash could occur in Soviet policy for the simple reason that all the Soviet leaders were agreed in believing that the survival of the Soviet regime in Russia was bound up with the success of the revolution in the rest of the world, or at any rate in Europe.

Mr. Hill, in common with most recent writers, exaggerates the difference between Lenin and Trotsky on this point, and makes one of his few serious mistakes when, having quoted Trotsky's remark that " either the Russian revolution will cause a revolution in the west, or the capitalists of all countries will strangle our revolution ", he adds that Lenin would never have committed himself to such a statement. Half a dozen statements of the same tenor can be found in Lenin's works, of which one, precisely contemporaneous with that of Trotsky, may be quoted as a sample :

Anglo-French and American imperialism will *inevitably* strangle the independence and freedom of Russia *unless* world-wide socialism, world-wide Bolshevism triumphs.

Lenin: The Master Builder

And in the purely hypothetical event of a clash, Lenin gave the same answer as Trotsky and in no less categorical terms. " He is no socialist ", Lenin wrote after Brest-Litovsk, " who will not sacrifice his fatherland for the triumph of the social revolution."

The debate between Lenin and Trotsky over Brest-Litovsk turned therefore on a question of timing and tactics rather than of principle, since the same premise was common to both. Bitterly as it was contested, it led imperceptibly to a kind of synthesis between national and international aspects of Soviet policy; for while Trotsky supported his case for staking everything on world revolution (or, more specifically, on revolution in Germany) by the argument, which Lenin at this time fully accepted, that without such a revolution the Soviet regime in Russia could not survive, Lenin, on his side, argued that nothing would be so certainly fatal to the cause of revolution in Germany as the overthrow of the Soviet republic by German imperialism, and that to defend and strengthen the Soviet regime by a prudent national policy was the surest ultimate guarantee of international revolution. Lenin was right. But the irony of the situation is that he was right for a reason which contradicted the premise accepted both by Trotsky and by himself — namely, the dependence of the survival of the regime in Russia on revolution elsewhere.

The synthesis established at the time of Brest-Litovsk between national and international policy, between the interests of the Soviet republic and those

Studies in Revolution

of world revolution, proved lasting. A whole generation of communists — Russian and foreign — was nurtured on the dual conception of the promotion of world revolution as the ultimate and necessary crown and reinforcement of the Soviet republic, and of the strengthening of Soviet power as the immediate and necessary spearhead of world revolution. The attempt to drive a wedge between these two facets of policy and exalt Lenin's realism in foreign policy at the expense of his loyalty to world revolution is misleading and mistaken. After Lenin's retirement from the scene, when it became clear that the prospects of the world revolution were, to say the least, far more remote than Lenin or any of his colleagues had dreamed, fresh strains were put on the synthesis. But though the balance was disturbed it was never broken. It remained reasonably possible nearly thirty years later to argue, as Lenin had argued over Brest-Litovsk, that the survival and strength of the Soviet State were the best pledge for the socialist revolution in other countries.

It has become a commonplace to praise Lenin's realism, his flexibility, his practical common sense in judging what could and what could not be done at the given moment; and all these qualities he possessed in a pre-eminent degree. But perhaps the most vivid impression left by a re-reading of his major works is of the amazing intellectual power and consistency of purpose which runs through them. His tactical readiness to compromise, to tack, to retreat when it became necessary was an enormous

Lenin: The Master Builder

asset to the politician. But what is infinitely more striking is that he seems to have known from the first where he was going and how he intended to get there, and that when he died in 1924 the revolution was firmly established on foundations which he had begun to dig thirty years before.

Lenin was clear from the outset that to make the revolution it was necessary to make a party. Virtually the whole of his active life before 1917 was devoted to this task. " There can be no revolutionary action ", he wrote in *What is to be Done?* " without a revolutionary theory "; and revolutionary theory dictated the character of the revolutionary party. As against the Narodniks the party was conceived by Lenin as a party of the proletariat; as against the " legal Marxists " as a party of action as well as of theory; as against the " economists " (the Russian counterpart of the " syndicalists " in the west) as a party with a political as well as an economic programme. Above all, it must be a party with a single mind and purpose: " if unity of view collapses, the party collapses ".

It was in the light of this doctrine that Lenin split the party, almost at the moment of its birth, by separating " Bolsheviks " from " Mensheviks ", and was prepared again and again during the next twenty years to sacrifice numbers to rigid discipline and unity. The only important compromise admitted by Lenin — his concession to the peasants — was dictated by the need of adapting what was originally a western doctrine to an eastern country where the peasantry formed more than 80 per cent

Studies in Revolution

of the population. But even this policy bore the marks of a strict and unbending consistency. It first took shape at the Stockholm congress of the party in 1906, when Lenin found it tactically necessary to retreat from the logical programme of nationalization and large-scale cultivation of the land. It continued in 1917, when Lenin took over the programme of the Social-Revolutionaries and made it the basis of the agrarian decree of the Soviet Government. It was carried to its logical conclusion in 1921, with the New Economic Policy. But, for all these compromises, Lenin never abandoned the two essential points that the leadership of the revolution rested with the proletariat (and this, among other reasons, presupposed a policy of industrialization as the *sine qua non* of a socialist order), and that the revolution could be carried into the countryside only by splitting the peasantry and raising the potentially revolutionary " poor peasant " against the petty bourgeois *kulak*. Collectivization was the logical and ultimate triumph of Lenin's agrarian policy, which he did not live to see.

Of the founder of every great religion, philosophy or political movement it is customary to say that he would have been horrified by much that was done by his disciples in his name. The statement is usually made meaningless in its application to a dynamic world by the assumption that the ideas of the founder remain static at the point where he left them. The curious compound of consistency and flexibility — or, as the critic might put it, of dogmatism and of opportunism — which marks Soviet

Lenin: *The Master Builder*

history is already inherent in the thoughts and writings of Lenin. But much has happened since Lenin died in 1924 in his fifty-fourth year and with his work only half done; and when Mr. Hill says, in his concluding chapter, "it is Lenin's words, Lenin's ideas, which are really authoritative in the Soviet Union to-day", he raises the whole controversy that centres round the name and achievement of Stalin.

10

SOREL: PHILOSOPHER OF SYNDICALISM

BORN at Cherbourg on November 2, 1847, Georges Sorel was, from the early twenties to the age of forty-five, a blameless *ingénieur des ponts-et-chaussées*. Then in 1892 he abandoned his profession to devote himself to his newly found hobby of writing about socialism. He helped to found two reviews and contributed to many more, wrote several books (of which one, *Reflections on Violence* — the only one of his works to be translated into English — enjoyed a *succès de scandale*) and became the recognized philosopher of the French trade-union or "syndicalist" movement. He died in August 1922 at Boulogne-sur-Seine, where he had spent the last twenty-five years of his uneventful life.

Sorel wrote — or at any rate published — nothing till he was in the forties; his masterpiece was written at fifty-nine, and he wrote with undiminished vigour till well on in his sixties. His late maturity gives a peculiar shape to his career. His formative years covered two intellectual generations; he wrote primarily for a third. He stands, a solitary and daring pioneer, at the most important cross-

152

Sorel: Philosopher of Syndicalism

roads of modern social and political thought. Born a few weeks before the *Communist Manifesto* and living on till the eve of the " march on Rome ", he looks back to Marx and Nietzsche (of the great thinkers who, more than anyone, undermined the foundations of bourgeois society and bourgeois morality — Marx, Nietzsche and Dostoevsky — Sorel missed only the third) and forward to Lenin, to the neo-Catholicism of Bloy and Péguy, and to Mussolini. There is no conceivable parallel in any other country to Sorel, except perhaps Bernard Shaw, ten years his junior in age, his contemporary in literary apprenticeship. But this parallel breaks down in at least one respect: Sorel was no artist and not even a very good writer.

Marx was Sorel's first master. He states in his *Confessions* that he was an orthodox Marxist till 1897; and this is as nearly true as it could be of one who was temperamentally incapable of bowing the knee to any orthodoxy. His starting-point, according to his own statement, was to discover " how the essential of the Marxist doctrines could be realized ". He drew largely from Nietzsche, in part directly, in part through Bergson, the philosopher of *L'Evolution créatrice* and the *élan vital*. The other, though less important, literary influence was Renan. Sorel wittily describes Renan as one of those French writers — he also counts Molière and Racine among them — who have eschewed profundity for fear of being excluded from the *salons* of their female admirers. But it was from Renan's belief in religious dogma as " a necessary imposture " that he derived

Studies in Revolution

his famous conception of the socialist " myth ".

The study of Sorel reveals unexpectedly numerous points of contact between Marx and Nietzsche. It is often puzzling whether Sorel's thought should be described as Marx reflected through a Nietzschean prism, or vice versa. But the dual influence, blended with an extreme subtlety, is always there, and colours all Sorel's fundamental beliefs.

The first article in Sorel's corrosive creed is derived equally from both his masters — his conviction of the decadence of bourgeois society. Sorel, one of his commentators has said, was literally haunted with the idea of decadence. *La Ruine du monde antique* was his first major work. The persistent attraction of Christianity for him is its dogma of original sin. The " princes of secular thought ", from Diderot onwards, are " philistines "; they bear (like Marx's " vulgar economists ") the hallmark of bourgeois culture — the belief in progress. *Les Illusions du progrès*, published in the same year as *Réflexions sur la violence*, is the most clearly and closely reasoned of his books.

Secondly, the rejection of the bourgeoisie and of bourgeois philosophy carries with it a revolt against the intellect. Sorel's earliest literary essay, *Le Procès de Socrate*, denounces Socrates for having corrupted civilization through the false doctrine that history moves forward through a process of intellectual inquiry and persuasion. This is the essence of the bourgeois heresy: " Est bourgeois ", in Alain's well-known aphorism, " tout ce qui vit de persuader." Like Marx, Sorel believes in

Sorel: Philosopher of Syndicalism

Nietzsche's (or rather, Pindar's) " eternal strife, father of all things ". Struggle and pain are the realities of life. Violence is the only cure for the evils of bourgeois civilization.

Thirdly, Sorel shares the common contempt of Nietzsche and Marx for bourgeois pacifism. In his specific glorification of war he harks back to Proudhon rather than to Marx (though Marx, in preaching class war, did not condemn national wars provided they were the right ones). Never, he remarks in *La Ruine du monde antique*, was there a great State so averse from war as the Roman Empire in its decadence. " In England the pacifist movement is closely connected with the chronic intellectual decadence which has overtaken that country." The surest symptom of the decay of the English bourgeoisie is its inability to take war seriously; English officers in South Africa (the date is 1900–01) " go to war like gentlemen to a football match ". The only alternative to a proletarian revolution as the creator of a new and healthy society would be a great European war; and this seemed to Sorel in the early 1900s a solution scarcely to be hoped for.

The fourth target of Sorel's animosity is bourgeois democracy. The case against bourgeois democracy has been so amply developed by others from the original Marxist premises that Sorel's contributions, though copious, are no longer specially significant:

Government by the mass of the citizens has never yet been anything but a fiction: yet this fiction was the

Studies in Revolution

last word of democratic science. No attempt has ever been made to justify this singular paradox by which the vote of a chaotic majority is supposed to produce what Rousseau calls the " general will " which is infallible.

Sorel's bitterness against democratic politics and democratic politicians was further sharpened by the *affaire Dreyfus*, when what had started as a noble campaign to vindicate justice was exploited for the mean ends of party or personal ambition. It was an error to look for noble aims in the masses. The majority, he had already declared in *Le Procès de Socrate*, " cannot in general accept great upheavals " ; they " cling to their traditions ". The audacious minority is always the instrument of change.

Sorel does not, however, remain merely destructive. His pessimism, he insists, is not the barren pessimism of the disillusioned optimist but the pessimism which, by accepting the decadence of the existing order, already constitutes " a step towards deliverance ". Yet while the goal is the goal of Marx, the voice is the voice of Nietzsche :

Socialism is a moral question in the sense that it brings into the world a new way of judging all human actions or, following a famous expression of Nietzsche, a transvaluation of all values. . . . The middle classes cannot find in their conditions of life any source of ideas which stand in direct opposition to bourgeois ideas ; the notion of catastrophe [Nietzsche called it " tragedy "] escapes them entirely. The proletariat, on the contrary, finds in its conditions of life something to nourish sentiments of solidarity and revolt ; it is in daily warfare with hierarchy and with property ; it can thus conceive moral values opposed to those consecrated by

Sorel: Philosopher of Syndicalism

tradition. In this transvaluation of all values by the militant proletariat lies the high originality of contemporary socialism.

The two moralities of Marx (proletarian morality and bourgeois morality) have oddly blended with the two moralities ("master" and "slave" morality) of Nietzsche. Sorel preached a "morality of producers" (among whom intellectuals were apparently not included); and in a further echo of the German philosopher he branded Christian morality as a "morality of mendicants". Curiously enough it was Jaurès, a favourite target of Sorel's ridicule, who made the apt remark that the proletarian was the contemporary superman.

Such is the basis of Sorel's cult of "revolutionary syndicalism". Syndicalism is, in Sorel's eyes, the true heir of Marxism. It is anti-political in two senses, both of them Marxist. In the first place it rejects the State, as Marx did and as most contemporary Marxists did not; it seeks not to capture the machinery of the State — much less to find places for socialist ministers in bourgeois governments — but to destroy it. Secondly, it asserts, as Marx did, the essential primacy of economics over politics. Political action is not class action: only economic action can be truly revolutionary. The *syndicats*, the trade unions, being not political parties but organizations of the workers, are alone capable of such action.

Revolutionary syndicalism, the economic action of the workers, can take the form only of the strike, and of the most absolute form of strike, the general strike, which had been a central point in the French

Studies in Revolution

syndicalist programme since 1892. A sworn enemy of all Utopias, Sorel refuses to draw any picture at all of the social order which will follow this health-giving outburst of proletarian violence. He borrows a phrase from Bernstein, the German " revisionist " who, from a different point of view, also laboured to purge Marxism of its Utopian ingredients: " The end is nothing, the movement is all ". And if critics drew attention to the motivelessness of the general strike so conceived, Sorel boldly rejected this excursion into rationalism. The general strike was not a rational construction, but the " myth " of socialism, necessary like the dogmas of the Christian Church and, like them, above rational criticism.

This famous Sorelian concept of the myth involves two significant consequences. The first is a purely relativist and pragmatic view of truth which in his earlier writings he had vigorously rejected. The myth is not something which is true in any abstract sense, but something in which it is useful to believe: this is indeed the meaning of truth. From the implied pragmatism of Bergson Sorel went on to the avowed pragmatism of William James and the American school. The last of all his writings was *De l'utilité du pragmatisme*, published in 1921.

The other consequence, which Sorel faced less clearly, was an " aristocratic " view of the movement which was asked to accept this philosophy. The syndicalist movement was to be based on a myth devised and propagated by an *élite* of leaders and enthusiastically accepted by the rank and file.

Sorel: Philosopher of Syndicalism

Such a view accorded well with Sorel's long-standing rejection of democracy and belief in " audacious minorities ". But it was not an easy view to fit into the principles and programmes of the CGT. The rift between the syndicalist movement in France and syndicalist philosophy elaborated for it by Sorel and his disciples was never really bridged.

It was perhaps some dim consciousness of the unreality of his position which brought Sorel to an intellectual crisis in 1910. It was a lean year in the history of socialism. It marked the nadir of the fortunes of Bolshevism; and even Lenin fell a prey to some discouragement. What is more to the present point, it was in this year that Benedetto Croce, who had hailed syndicalism as " a new form of Marx's great dream, dreamed a second time by Georges Sorel ", declared that socialism, whether in its old Marxist or its new Sorelian form, was " dead ". Sorel, in his sixty-third year but still at the height of his powers, was too restless a spirit to resign himself to defeat. His main work had been done. But the turn which he now took is of immense significance in assessing his ultimate influence. Of the three paths which led forward from the cross-roads at which Sorel stood — Neo-Catholicism, Bolshevism and Fascism — all were tentatively explored by Sorel himself. But he followed none of them to the end.

One of the more baffling by-products of the *affaire Dreyfus* had been the formation of a tiny group of which the moving spirit was a young Dreyfusard, the self-taught son of a peasant, Charles Péguy. It

Studies in Revolution

centred round a modest periodical, *Les Cahiers de la Quinzaine*, edited, and for the most part written, by Péguy himself. Contrary to all the traditions of the *affaire*, Péguy was strongly nationalist, pro-Catholic, anti-democratic and a hater of the bourgeoisie. Since 1902 Sorel had written occasional papers for the *Cahiers*, had attended the weekly Thursdays of the group, and had been accepted as its "elder statesman" and mentor. Through this group Sorel elaborated the idea of a reconciliation between French syndicalism and French nationalism. His first contribution to the *Cahiers* had borne the significant title, "Socialismes nationaux": its theme was that "there are at least as many socialisms as there are great nations".

French nationalism was at this time scarcely thinkable outside the framework of Catholicism, and it was therefore logical, though surprising, that Sorel and his syndicalist disciple Berth should in 1910 have formed, in alliance with three members of the *Action Française*, a group which they called *La Cité Française*, to publish a periodical under the title *L'Indépendance Française*; and in the same year Sorel wrote in *Action Française* (his sole contribution to the journal) an appreciation of Péguy's *Mystère de la charité de Jeanne d'Arc*. The whole enterprise, the form of which changed in 1912 to a "Cercle Proudhon", was short-lived; the cohabitation was never easy. But the break came in 1913, not from Sorel but from Péguy.

The causes of the rupture are obscure, and Péguy may have suffered from persecution mania. But it

Sorel: Philosopher of Syndicalism

seems clear that Peguy, young, devout and austere, could not in the long run accommodate himself to a philosophy which enthusiastically hailed the dogmas of the Church as necessary myths. Nevertheless, when Péguy died on the Marne in September 1914, it was in that firm faith in war as the means of salvation for a decadent French society which Sorel had held from the outset of his career. No study either of the movement represented by the *Cahiers de la Quinzaine* or of the revival of French nationalism in general in the decade before 1914 can ignore the author of *Réflexions sur la violence*. It is these years which have led Sorel's able German biographer, Michael Freund, to give his book the inept sub-title, " Revolutionary Conservatism "

The story of Sorel's affinities with Bolshevism is less complex and probably less important. The documents are at least unequivocal. Lenin was a sworn enemy of syndicalism, which he regarded as tantamount to anarchism. He had no faith in the all-sufficiency of the general strike. He believed firmly in political as well as economic action; and, though he was more deeply committed before 1917 than after to the ultimate denial of the State, he was convinced that a political dictatorship of the proletariat was the immediate goal of revolution. He seems to have mentioned Sorel only once in his published works, dismissing him curtly as " muddle-headed " and his writings as " senseless ". Nobody familiar with the clear logic of Lenin's own thought will find the verdict surprising.

Sorel, on the other hand, welcomed the October

Studies in Revolution

revolution with open arms. For five years he had written scarcely anything. The war, begun as a war for the French nation, which he loved, was being more and more widely hailed as a war for democracy, which he loathed. Here was a long-awaited breath of fresh air — a revolution which preached and practised a salutary violence, spat on bourgeois democracy, exalted the " morality of the producer ", *alias* the proletariat, and installed Soviets as autonomous organs of self-government. Moreover, the Bolshevik Party — had Sorel cared to note the fact — was built up precisely on the Sorelian premises of an " audacious minority " leading the instinctive proletarian mass.

Sorel made no formal declaration of adhesion to the new cause and creed. But he wrote several articles for the French *Revue Communiste*; and in 1920, when Bolshevism was at the height of its unpopularity in France, he added to the fourth edition of *Réflexions sur la violence* a " plaidoyer pour Lénine " in which he hailed the Russian revolution as " the red dawn of a new epoch ".

Before descending into the tomb [concluded the " plaidoyer "] may I see the humiliation of the arrogant bourgeois democracies, to-day so cynically triumphant.

Bolshevism was not yet prosperous enough to ignore its few distinguished friends, even if they were not wholly orthodox. After Sorel died the *Communist International*, the official journal of Comintern, opened its columns to a lengthy, if critical, appreciation of this " reactionary petty-bourgeois Proudhonist and

Sorel: Philosopher of Syndicalism

anarcho-syndicalist " who had rallied to the defence of the proletarian revolution.

> Sorel [concluded the article] for all his mistakes has helped, and will continue to help, the development of the will to revolution, rightly understood, and of proletarian activity in the struggle for Communism.

The facts of Sorel's relations with Fascism are also beyond dispute. Italy always held a special place in his affections; in no other foreign country were his works so widely read, admired and translated. The shabby treatment of Italy by the peacemakers at Versailles had deepened his resentment at the triumph of bourgeois democracy. His writings teem with anticipations of Fascist doctrine. " What I am ", said Mussolini himself, " I owe neither to Nietzsche nor to William James, but to Georges Sorel." Georges Valois, one of the *Action Française* group which collaborated with Sorel in 1910, called him admiringly the " intellectual father of Fascism "; and his first biographer was Lanzillo, the Italian Fascist. He praised the first achievements of Fascism. But when the Fascist revolution brought Mussolini to Rome, Sorel was already dead.

What Sorel would have thought of the Fascist regime in power is an unprofitable, though inevitable, speculation. When he praised the first Fascists in a letter to Croce it was because " their violence is an advantageous substitute for the might of the State " — a modern equivalent of the Mafia and the Camorra, whose extra-legal activities and organization had always fascinated him. He saw in

Studies in Revolution

Fascism a realization of the syndicalist dream of an administrative power independent of the State. The question which Sorel died without having to answer was that of his attitude to the totalitarian State. All his life he had been a strong, almost violent, individualist; all his life he had fought, not for the concentration of power but for its dispersal and decentralization to the very limit of anarchism. At the very end of his life he argued against any absolute religious belief on the ground that it could not be successfully propagated without restoring the Inquisition. It would have been disconcerting — to say the least — to find Sorel as a prophet of totalitarianism. But his thought contains too many inconsistencies, his career too many unexpected turns, for anyone to pronounce with assurance on this hypothetical question.

But the most interesting point raised by Sorel's career is that of the resemblances and differences between Bolshevism and Fascism. If Sorel stands on the common ground where Marx and Nietzsche meet, this is also the common ground from which Bolshevism and Fascism diverge. Marx and Nietzsche, Bolshevism and Fascism, both deny bourgeois democracy with its bourgeois interpretations of liberty and equality; both reject the bourgeois doctrines of persuasion and compromise; both (though this is where Sorel held aloof from both) proclaim absolutes which command the obedience of the individual at the cost of all else.

There was, however, an essential difference. The absolute of Nietzsche and of Fascism ends

Sorel : Philosopher of Syndicalism

with the super-man or the super-nation or simply with power as a good in itself and for its own sake. Marx and Bolshevism propound a universal end in the form of the good of the proletariat of all countries, in which the whole of mankind is ultimately merged ; and the ideal stands, whatever shortcomings may be encountered in the pursuit of it. Sorel, while clear enough about what he rejected, never committed himself on the positive side. That, among other reasons, is why he has left no school or party, even among the syndicalists whom he sought to serve and teach. He cannot be assigned either to Bolshevism or to Fascism (and still less to the Catholics). Sorel's thought is not a beacon — or even a candle — throwing a steady beam within a defined radius ; it is rather a prism reflecting, fitfully but brilliantly, the most penetrating political insights of his day and of our own.

11

MR. GALLACHER AND THE CPGB

DESERT and accident have combined to make Mr. William Gallacher the most representative British Communist. He was in the thick of all the frays out of which the Communist Party of Great Britain (CPGB) was born; he was a delegate at the second congress of the Communist International in Moscow in the summer of 1920, when the main lines of guidance for the then embryonic CPGB were laid down; he has been a regular member of the central committee of the party and of its Politbureau; and he was an M.P. for three or four times as long as any other member of the party, having sat for West Fife as a Communist for 15 years. It is not, therefore, surprising that he should have been invited to write a companion volume in the " Penguin " series to the recent volumes on the Labour and Conservative Parties, *The Case for Communism*. His previous writings consist of two volumes of reminiscences, *Revolt on the Clyde*, published in the 1930s, and *The Rolling of the Thunder*, published in 1947.[1]

[1] William Gallacher, *The Case for Communism*. (Penguin Special.) Penguin Books. 1s. 6d. *The Rolling of the Thunder*. Second Impression. Lawrence and Wishart. 5s.

Mr. Gallacher and the CPGB

The CPGB was the product of a marriage between haphazard British initiative and strict Leninist discipline. The first world war multiplied and stimulated the various groups of the extreme Left, especially on the Clyde, always the home both of Left-wingisms and of stubborn and unruly labour movements. The first Russian revolution of February 1917 evoked a wave of enthusiasm. Ramsay MacDonald and Philip Snowden were among the sponsors of a famous meeting at Leeds in the summer of 1917, which decided to establish Workers' and Soldiers' Councils throughout Great Britain and appointed a committee to carry out the decision. The October revolution further stimulated the left wing of the Labour movement, but drove a wedge between it and the centre, especially as the anti-war attitude of the Left became more pronounced, agitation for social revolution to stop the war took the place of the vague pacifist idealism of earlier pronouncements. Reality was given to this agitation by industrial unrest, of which the Clyde was once more the centre. After the armistice it flared up on "Red Friday", January 31, 1919, when there was a battle between strikers and police in George Square, Glasgow, and a red flag was run up on the city flag-pole. Mr. Gallacher and Mr. Shinwell were among those who were arrested and received sentences of imprisonment for their share in these proceedings.

Out of the anti-war movement two main parties with more or less openly revolutionary programmes had emerged — the British Socialist Party and the

Studies in Revolution

Socialist Labour Party; other groups of a similar character flourished in particular localities. The strongly pacifist Left wing of the ILP contained many fellow-travellers; and the Plebs League, a group of intellectuals interested in the education of the workers in Marxist doctrine, formed the theoretical spearhead of the movement. On another front the rapidly developing shop-stewards' movement had a marked revolutionary colour. It was opposed both to the old trade-union leadership and to parliamentary action in general; though varying in outlook from place to place and from time to time, it was syndicalist in character and tended to advocate " direct action " without any very clear definition of political purposes. It was with this movement, collectively known as the Workers' Committee Movement, that Mr. Gallacher was at this time primarily associated.

The founding of the Third or Communist International in Moscow in March 1919 had little immediate impact on these groups. It was the second congress of Comintern in July 1920 which proved the decisive force in the creation of the British party. The party was officially founded in London on July 31, 1920, while the Moscow congress was actually in progress. But the real arguments which moulded its shape and destiny were conducted in Moscow, where Lenin presided over a commission to advise on the affairs of the new party. The British Left was more amply represented at this than at any other congress of Comintern; and in those formative years a latitude and diversity of

Mr. Gallacher and the CPGB

opinion was still tolerated. Quelch and MacLaine, both of the British Socialist Party, represented a "joint provisional committee" for the creation of a British Communist Party; Murphy, the Socialist Labour Party; Gallacher, Tanner and Ramsay, the shop-stewards' movement; and Sylvia Pankhurst a small independent group which had tried to get in first by appropriating the name of "British Communist Party".

Lenin's policy at this time was to rally all the forces of the extreme Left against the orthodox parties of Social-Democratic or Labour complexion which had supported their respective national Governments during the war, and could therefore be considered as having sold themselves irretrievably to the bourgeoisie. Thus, while opposed to any co-operation with such parties, he was tolerant of the many differences dividing the extreme Left and anxious only to bring them together in united Communist parties. Mr. Gallacher begins the second instalment of his autobiography with the story how, on arriving in Petrograd on his way to the second congress of the Communist International, he had thrust into his hand the English edition of Lenin's newly published pamphlet, *The Infantile Disorder of "Leftism" in Communism*, and found himself indicted by name as a victim of this disease on the ground of his opposition to parliamentary action.

At the congress itself Lenin was ranged with the two delegates of the British Socialist Party, who formed the Right wing of the British group, against Mr. Gallacher and the other British delegates in

Studies in Revolution

support of the thesis that the future Communist Party of Great Britain should take part in parliamentary elections and seek affiliation to the Labour Party. It is piquant that Britain's future Communist M.P. should have gone on record as declaring that Communists " have something better to do than waste time over parliamentary elections ". But Mr. Gallacher, having been out-voted, allowed himself to be won over by Lenin's persuasive personality, and went home promising not only to carry out the majority policy but to dissuade his Scottish friends from indulging their nationalist feelings so far as to found a separate Scottish Communist Party. The news of the foundation of the CPGB reached Moscow while the congress was in progress. It was due in part to Mr. Gallacher's efforts that it secured the adhesion of all the main Left-wing groups north and south of the Border. The formal constitution of the party was approved at a conference at Leeds in January 1921. Arthur MacManus was elected president (a post which has long since disappeared); Mr. Gallacher was the runner-up.

The history of the first years of the CPGB has yet to be written. In the 1930s an attempt was made by one of its founders and its first national organizer, Tom Bell. But his work was subjected in party circles to charges, not unfounded, of inaccuracy and distortion; and nobody has since been bold enough to repeat the experiment. The author of *The Rolling of the Thunder* has no claim to be a historian. But as a participant in every stage of party history he is an important witness. His particular contribution

Mr. Gallacher and the CPGB

is to fit party affairs into the framework of British Labour and trade-union history during this period, and thus to rebut the stereotyped charge that party policies were dictated from Moscow. Mr. Gallacher is a sturdy Scot, and nobody will suspect him of taking orders or of allowing himself to be persuaded against his will. But the founding of the party in 1920 was not the only occasion on which the casting vote of Moscow was decisive in divisions and disputes between British Communists. The very weakness of the party made the tutelage of Moscow inevitable, even where it was not deliberately imposed or consciously accepted.

The initial dilemma which faced the CPGB faced virtually every other Communist party throughout the twenty years after 1919, and was indeed the fundamental problem of Comintern. Was the party to remain small, highly organized and disciplined, and doctrinally impeccable — as Lenin's Bolsheviks had been before 1917 — even at the cost of exercising no present influence on national affairs and becoming, if necessary, an illegal and persecuted sect? Or was it to seek to become a mass party playing an active role in national politics, even at the cost of loosened discipline and organization and a certain measure of doctrinal eclecticism or, at any rate, toleration? Neither Lenin nor the other Bolshevik leaders ever fully understood the dilemma confronting the Communists in the western democracies — a dilemma which had no counterpart in Russia. Thus the Comintern resolutions of 1920 enjoined the nascent

171

Studies in Revolution

British Communist Party to play an active part in British parliamentary democracy and to seek affiliation to the Labour Party. But they also imposed on it, in common with other Communist parties, a rigid organization subject to " iron discipline " and periodical purges of the unruly, as well as to acceptance of all decisions of the Communist International; and they required it not only to conduct propaganda for the establishment of the dictatorship of the proletariat but to create an underground organization in preparation for civil war. Nobody in Moscow seems to have realized that these were incompatible alternatives.

Of all the Communist parties the CPGB was the only one which, thanks in part to peculiar British conditions, in part perhaps to its share of the famous British genius for compromise, seriously attempted the impossible. The membership of the CPGB after its congress of January 1921 amounted to not more than 2000 or 2500; the total of 10,000 announced at the third congress of Comintern that year and repeated by Mr. Gallacher was obtained, as Bell admits, by adding up the wishful estimates of half-organized branches. On the other hand, the " Hands off Russia " movement and the Councils of Action in the last stages of the Russian civil war had revealed a vast mass of vague sympathy with Soviet Russia and her institutions. This sympathy was strongly tinged with pacifism and hostility to war in general, and did not betoken revolutionary convictions. But few — and, least of all, the Communists — recognized these limitations; and to create a dis-

Mr. Gallacher and the CPGB

ciplined Communist Party on Moscow lines with a mass following did not seem a hopeless task.

The first blow was the blank rejection by the Labour Party of the application for affiliation — a rejection three times repeated and endorsed by an enormous majority at the annual conference in 1921. The CPGB showed apparently sincere surprise at the decision, and expressed a keen sense of grievance, which is reflected in Mr. Gallacher's pages, at the unfriendly Labour attitude. But this was surely an inevitable result of the equivocal position of the Communists themselves. It was at the second congress of the Communist International that Lenin coined the famous recommendation to "support the Labour Party as the rope supports the man who is being hanged" — an aphorism which an English Communist is said to have translated as "taking them by the hand as a preliminary to taking them by the throat". Alliance with the Labour Party could never be more than a tactical device, a stage on the road to the dictatorship of the proletariat. At the moment when the alliance was being offered, the Communists were already seeking to undermine Labour authority in the trade unions through such organizations as the Minority Movement and the National Unemployed Workers' Movement; and it was not surprising that the alliance should have been consistently rejected by the Labour Party leadership. Indeed, the Communist assault from the Left was one of the factors which drove moderate Labour parties to seek an open or covert bourgeois alliance.

Studies in Revolution

These inconsistencies within the CPGB were, however, complicated by violent zigzags of policy in Comintern itself. Delays in the realization of European revolution, the introduction of NEP, the opening up of trade relations with the capitalist world, all brought a certain mitigation of Moscow's uncompromising hostility to the non-communist world. In December 1921 the Executive Committee of Comintern (ECCI) for the first time issued the slogan of a " united front " with other working-class parties and support for " Labour Governments "; and three months later the CPGB was specifically instructed to " establish relations " with the General Council of the TUC and to apply once more for admission to the Labour Party. This blind persistence merely courted another snub. The 1922 conference of the Labour Party at Edinburgh produced more plain speaking at the expense of the Communists than ever before. This time the party could not fail to perceive that something was seriously wrong. On Mr. Gallacher's proposal a committee of three non-official members of the party — Mr. Harry Pollitt, a trade unionist, Mr. Palme Dutt, an intellectual, and Harry Inkpin, brother of the secretary of the party — was appointed to report on its affairs.

The results of this report were far-reaching. The party was reorganized on the model of the Russian party, discipline was tightened, and it was decided to refrain from electoral attacks on the Labour Party. These changes yielded some dividends. In 1923 two Communists, Newbold and Saklatvala,

Mr. Gallacher and the CPGB

standing for constituencies where there was no Labour candidate, were elected to Parliament with unofficial Labour support.

This tacit alliance was, however, never welcomed or sanctioned by the Labour leaders, and its artificiality was quickly demonstrated. What proved fatal to it was the accession of Labour to power in January 1924. The CPGB could, at the cost of some mutual embarrassment, support a Labour Opposition; it could not conceivably support a Labour Government. Relations were soon worse than ever. The London conference of the Labour Party in 1924 took steps to exclude Communists from individual membership of any branch of the party, though they could still come into it as members of affiliated trade unions. The ultimate crisis arose, logically enough, out of the British general strike. This was the parting of the ways between those who wanted revolution and those who rejected revolution. It quickly became clear that the majority of those who had embarked on the general strike were not prepared to cross the Rubicon which separates strike from revolution, even if by holding back they brought about the defeat of the strikers.

The Communists, applauded and backed up by Moscow, denounced the retreat as treachery to the working class, but thereby only revealed their own isolation. The prestige of the CPGB, as well as that of the Soviet Government, underwent a severe slump. In the early 1920s sympathy with Soviet Russia among the Labour rank-and-file had not only tempered official Labour hostility to the Com-

175

Studies in Revolution

munists but had put an effective brake on official action against Soviet Russia. Now only the feeblest of protests followed the Arcos raid and the breaking off of relations with the Soviet Union in 1927. Under the first Baldwin Government, with Joynson Hicks as Home Secretary, anti-Communist feeling reached its height. According to the figures quoted by Mr. Gallacher, the party membership fell from 11,000–12,000 after the general strike to 5000 in the following year.

These disasters led to a second reorganization of the CPGB in the winter of 1927–28. The policy of supporting the Labour Party against the bourgeois parties, equivocal though it was, and inconsistently as it had been pursued, had been an official plank in the party platform ever since its foundation and rested on the mandate given to the party by Lenin himself. The majority of the central committee, including Mr. Gallacher himself, saw no reason to change this policy. But a minority, led by Mr. Palme Dutt and Mr. Pollitt, now challenged it as wrong in principle. They argued that the situation in Great Britain had changed radically since Lenin made his recommendations of 1920. The economic position of Great Britain was deteriorating and therefore bringing nearer the objective conditions for a mass revolutionary movement; the Labour Party had been in office and had revealed itself as " a third bourgeois party "; and it had in effect abandoned the loose and undogmatic federal structure, which had made it seem possible for Communists to seek admission to it, in favour of a

176

Mr. Gallacher and the CPGB

centralized organization which was being used to impose the views of the leadership and to ban the Communists. On these grounds open opposition to Labour as to other parties was recommended as the right tactics for the CPGB.

The split in the central committee was taken to Moscow for settlement at a moment when Comintern was being rocked by a major crisis over the affairs of China. The occasion provided an admirable illustration of the results of the assumption, habitually made at Comintern headquarters, of a doctrinal and tactical uniformity applicable to all Communist parties. The collapse of the Anglo-Russian Joint Trade Union Council in 1926, after little more than a year of life, had already caused perturbation in Comintern circles and prepared the way for a swing to the Left. When, however, ECCI met in February 1928 to consider the British issue, many other things had happened. Trotsky had just been expelled from the party and banished to Alma Ata; and, after six months of embittered debate, the new " Left " policy in China of out-and-out opposition to Chiang Kai-shek had just been put in operation. Thus the views of Mr. Dutt and Mr. Pollitt, and not those of the majority, fitted in with the prevailing temper at headquarters. The ruling went in their favour. For tactical reasons, the CPGB was to maintain " the slogan of affiliation to the Labour Party ". In all other respects the break was to be complete.

This decision, which was general rather than particular, marked a fateful new turn in Comintern

Studies in Revolution

policy as a whole. From 1928 onwards, and especially after the sixth congress held in August of that year, it became the fashion to treat Labour and Social-Democrat Parties not merely as declared enemies, but as the worst enemies, of the workers; and this line, pursued to its logical conclusion, had fatal consequences in Germany during the period of Hitler's ascent to power. Mr. Gallacher, who is too good a party man to defend his own stand in 1927-28 (he does not even refer to it), admits the error of the German Communists in the early 1930s, though he makes out a case for assigning an equal share of blame to the Social-Democrats. The dilemma which had dogged the steps of the CPGB from the outset proved an equally insuperable obstacle to the unity of the German Left.

In Britain the chief result of the 1928 decision was the retirement of Albert Inkpin, the secretary of the party since its inception. He was succeeded by Mr. Pollitt, who has been its virtual leader for the past twenty years. The history of the CPGB under Mr. Pollitt's leadership has been less turbulent and less eventful than in the preceding eight years of its existence. Technically the party has been much more efficiently run. The *Daily Worker* dates from 1930. Sharp changes of policy, even sudden changes, have occurred. But the party line, however vulnerable, has always been clear and precise, and has always responded to directives from Moscow. On the other hand, thoughts of a mass party have been abandoned or relegated to an indeterminate future. The influx of members into the party in

Mr. Gallacher and the CPGB

the " united front " period of the middle 1930s was largely unsolicited. This was no longer the " united front " with Labour in the old sense, but a diplomatic alliance, irrespective of opinions, between all who were willing to fight Hitler. What was wanted was not primarily converts to Communism, but converts to a policy of active resistance to German aggression. The same was true of the period after 1941, when the party received another substantial but transient accession of membership.

Mr. Gallacher's autobiography does not throw much light on events within the party after 1928; and, though he remained a member of the central committee and of its Politbureau, it may be inferred that he took little part in shaping policy. He had already on several occasions stood as a candidate for Scottish constituencies and come out at the bottom of the poll; the first was the Dundee election of 1922 when Mr. Churchill ran third to E. D. Morel and Scrymgeour, the prohibitionist. In 1935 Mr. Gallacher was elected as a Communist for the mining constituency of West Fife, and re-elected ten years later. In the House of Commons he won popularity and respect as a good parliamentarian. In the CPGB he represents, not the esoteric side of party life but its link with the masses; he has been for the past ten years its most important " public face ". He continues, within the limits of party discipline, to stand for the conception of the party as an extreme Left wing within the British parliamentary system rather than as an entity standing outside, and in unqualified opposition to, that system.

Studies in Revolution

Something of this attitude tinges even the cautious and carefully balanced pages of *The Case for Communism*. As a popular exposition of Marxist theory and of the economic aims, immediate and ultimate, of Socialism and Communism, this could not be bettered either in matter or in style. But when it comes to the political instruments for translating theory into practice and realizing economic ends, everything is suddenly vague and blurred. The dictatorship of the proletariat is lost altogether in the haze, and does not seem to be mentioned at all. The haze thickens to a fog in the last chapter, in which Mr. Gallacher returns some bewildering answers to questions from an imaginary critic. Here and there the reader even catches glimpses of an independent version of Communist doctrine and Communist tactics adapted to the demands of British politics. But this is surely a lost cause. Its development is inhibited by the slavish imitation of Soviet methods and of Soviet policies which has become endemic in the CPGB. The vicious circle cannot be broken. A more independent party would have shown greater health and strength; a healthier and stronger party would have achieved greater independence. The growth of the child has been fatally stunted by too successful and too masterful a parent.

12

THE REVOLUTION THAT FAILED

THE German Communist Party was one of the very few Communist parties other than the Russian which had independent roots of its own and was not a product of the Russian revolution or a child of the Communist International. Its pre-history began with the outbreak of the first world war. In August 1914 the German Social-Democrats, the largest, most powerful and best organized Marxist party in the world, were guilty of the great betrayal by voting for the German war budget — the symbol of support for the German national cause. A tiny handful of the party leaders, and perhaps a larger proportion of the rank and file, were against the decision. But party discipline demanded that the minority should accept the decision of the majority; it was not till December 1914 that Karl Liebknecht, and he alone, broke the party unity by voting against the war credits in the Reichstag.

As the war dragged on, opposition grew beneath the surface; and in 1916 there was a big break-away ending in the formation of the Independent Social-Democratic Party — the USPD, to use its German

Studies in Revolution

initials — which was against the war. Even the USPD was not really a revolutionary party. It wanted primarily to end the war, and found room for elements which were pacifist rather than Marxist. But it was within the USPD that there arose a group calling itself the *Spartakusbund*, which was out-and-out Marxist and revolutionary as well as anti-war, and came nearer than any other group in Germany to acceptance of Lenin's slogan of turning the imperialist war into a civil war of the proletariat against the bourgeois ruling class. The intellectual driving force of the *Spartakusbund* was Rosa Luxemburg; Karl Liebknecht, who was a leader and agitator rather than a theorist, was also one of the leaders of the group. The *Spartakusbund* and all its publications and activities were, of course, highly illegal in war-time Germany; both Liebknecht and Luxemburg spent the last months of the war in prison.

The *Spartakusbund* came into existence before the Russian revolution. But events in Russia gave its work a fresh impetus. At the end of December 1918, in the midst of the turmoil and upheaval which followed the armistice in Germany, a congress was held in Berlin. It was attended by Radek as a fraternal delegate from the central committee of the All-Russian Congress of Soviets: Zinoviev and Bukharin were also to have come, but were refused admission by the German Government. The congress decided to found a German Communist Party (KPD); and for old time's sake the name *Spartakusbund* was kept in brackets at the end of its name,

The Revolution that Failed

just as the Russians afterwards called themselves "Russian Communist Party (Bolsheviks)".

The *Spartakusbund* had been a small group composed mainly of intellectuals and engaged in propaganda, but not in active preparation for revolutionary action, which would indeed have been scarcely practicable during the war. When the KPD was created, the question arose whether it was to remain a small and highly concentrated party for the revolutionary indoctrination of the masses, or whether it was at once to go out for a mass membership and seek to become a mass revolutionary party. Liebknecht wanted the second course. Out of the chaos of post-armistice Berlin there had appeared a genuine workers' revolutionary movement, the shop-stewards' organization. It had, as yet, not spread beyond the capital. Its positive aims were not defined in very articulate terms. But it wanted social revolution and the overthrow of Ebert's Left coalition government, did not believe in parliamentary action and was prepared and organized to use force to attain its ends. If this group could be married to the *Spartakusbund*, a mass Communist Party, equally qualified for theory and for practice, was in sight.

This alliance was, however, opposed by Rosa Luxemburg, who believed that the masses were not yet ripe for a proletarian revolution, that a period of education and indoctrination was required, and that for this purpose a small party of agitators and propagandists on the model of the *Spartakusbund* was the right instrument; and the division among the

Studies in Revolution

leaders stultified the negotiations which Liebknecht carried on with the shop-stewards' movement during the founding congress of the KPD. The shop-stewards would have come in on terms, including parity of representation in the organs of the new party, which, considering the numbers they had behind them, was not unreasonable. But the old stalwarts of the *Spartakusbund* were obdurate and negotiations broke down. It was a decisive moment. Within a fortnight the Independent Social-Democrats had been ousted from the Ebert Government. Noske had become Minister of War with a mandate to use the Reichswehr to restore order in Berlin, and Liebknecht and Rosa Luxemburg had both been arrested and " shot while trying to escape " — one of the earliest uses of this famous euphemism for the official assassination of political opponents. Tragedy dogged the steps of German communism from the very outset.

Just two months after the foundation of the KPD in Berlin, the Communist International — Comintern — was born in Moscow. Rosa Luxemburg, who had regarded the creation of a mass Communist Party in Germany as premature, took the same view of the creation of a Communist International with world-wide pretensions; and this view was reinforced in German minds by the well-grounded fear that, if a Communist International were brought into being at a time when the German party was still a puling infant and the Russian party was the only one with a successful revolution to its credit, the centre of gravity would inevitably

The Revolution that Failed

be in Moscow and not in Berlin. Thus the German delegate, one Eberlein, appeared in Moscow in March 1919 with instructions to oppose the founding of the International. He found himself completely isolated among the delegates of the very real and active Russian Communist Party and of rudimentary and sometimes mythical communist organizations in such countries as the United States, Switzerland, Holland, Sweden, Norway, Hungary and Austria; and in the end, having stated his objections, he abstained from voting in order not to mar the universal harmony. But the fact remained that the Communist International had been created without the vote of the one potentially powerful Communist Party outside Russia, and of the one great industrial country where Marxist doctrine had a real hold on proletarian consciousness — a country on which all good Bolsheviks, from Lenin downwards, still pinned their confident hopes of a European revolution.

For the first eighteen months of its existence the KPD remained what the *Spartakusbund* had been during the war, a small, illegal, persecuted sect without any overt influence on events. Its outstanding figure at this time was Paul Levi, a brilliant and highly cultivated intellectual, but not in the least a political leader of the masses. The period after the roundation of Comintern in March 1919 was the time when contacts between Russian and German communists were at their lowest point. The year 1919 saw Soviet Russia almost entirely cut off from the rest of the world, and her leaders too preoccupied with the desperate struggle of the civil

Studies in Revolution

war to have much time or thought for anything not directly concerned with it. In Germany Radek had been arrested and imprisoned by the German authorities; no other leading Bolshevik came to take his place.

The KPD played no role in the famous Bavarian revolution of April 1919, though some communists joined the short-lived Soviet Government which was set up in Munich. It had only a walking-on part in the first attempted nationalist come-back after the humiliation of November 1918 — the so-called "Kapp putsch" of March 1920 — which was defeated, not by the communists but by a general strike organized by the old trade unions. But in the autumn of 1920, partly under Russian pressure, a split occurred among the German Independent Social-Democrats — the USPD. Under the combined influence of the prestige of Comintern and the eloquence of Zinoviev, who addressed a party congress at Halle for four hours on end, a majority of the USPD decided to join the communists to form the United Communist Party of Germany. There was thus, at the end of 1920, a mass German Communist Party with an effective membership of over 300,000 and a much larger number of fellow-travellers. But the unreality of the union between the intellectuals of the KPD and the workers of the USPD has been brilliantly portrayed by an eye-witness of the Berlin convention which ratified it:

There was an artistic frame of classical music and revolutionary poetry. The USPD delegates, mostly workers from the bench, were disgusted by the new

186

The Revolution that Failed

official pomp: they had looked forward to a sober analysis of the German situation, concrete proposals on what to do next. Paul Levi gave them instead a speech on the economic situation of the world, in which a wealth of statistics was combined with varied news of events in Asia and in the Anglo-American world, and which ended with the bombast, "Enter, ye workers of Germany, enter, for here are thy [*sic*] gods". I watched workers from Essen and Hamburg leaving the conference hall: they could express their disgust with this rhetoric only by despoiling some of the nice decorations with their plebeian spit.

For all the spitefulness of this account, there is truth in the picture of failure to unite the masses with the party leadership.

The book from which this quotation comes was published in the United States in 1948 under the rather misleading title, *Stalin and German Communism*. Its author, Ruth Fischer, is an Austrian who joined the KPD in 1919 and remained one of its leading members till her expulsion in 1926. For the story of the party during that time it is a primary source of great importance. It is, however, a source which the historian will have to handle with some care. Mrs. Fischer was in a position to know nearly everything that went on at this time in the inner counsels of the German Communist Party, and something — though not by any means all — of what went on in the Communist International. Her narrative is packed with detail; but, except where it is actually documented (as many of her statements are), it is often difficult to disentangle what rests on personal knowledge from hearsay and, even more, conjecture.

Studies in Revolution

Some of Mrs. Fischer's political speculations are not particularly convincing. One can rarely prove a negative. But it does not seem at all likely that Trotsky failed to return to Moscow in time for Lenin's funeral as the result of " a secret understanding with the Politburo " ; or that the famous " Zinoviev letter " which played a part in the British general election of 1924 was a forgery of the GPU ; or that J. D. Gregory, the British civil servant involved in the case, was in the pay of the GPU ; or that Dimitrov's defence in the Reichstag fire trial was a put-up job after a bargain for his release had been struck with his own cognizance between the GPU and the Gestapo.

The other qualification that must be made concerns Mrs. Fischer's political attitude. At first sight her reminiscences invite comparison with those of another woman who worked in Comintern in the early days and was bitterly disillusioned by the experience, Angelica Balabanoff. But they belong to different worlds. Balabanoff was a disappointed idealist who apparently did not know that Communist parties, like other political organizations, are not run without a great deal of wire-pulling, manipulation and sordid calculation of expediency. Mrs. Fischer was, from the outset, a politician to the finger-tips. If she became embittered, it was because she lost the last move in the game, not because she did not understand the game that was being played. In German party affairs she belonged to the Left, that is to say, to those communists who were opposed to temporary tactical

The Revolution that Failed

co-operation with the Social-Democrats, and believed that the workers could be directly organized for revolution. Writing twenty-five years later on the other side of the Atlantic, after her opinions have undergone a complete transformation, it can hardly be expected that she will have done full justice to her own position at the time — and still less to that of adversaries, who ousted her from the party leadership and against whom she has many old scores to work off.

The split between Right and Left in the KPD really dates from the so-called " March action " of 1921. In March of that year a spontaneous rising in the mining area of central Germany was followed by an attempted rising organized by the Communists in the great industrial centres. It seems to have been poorly prepared, and ended in defeat. The reprisals undertaken by the police and the Reichswehr were harsh, and left the party crippled, discredited and discouraged. Recriminations followed. According to one account, the " March action " was forced on reluctant leaders by the enthusiastic new recruits who had come into the party in the previous autumn. It is certainly true that Paul Levi had been forced to resign from the leadership a few weeks earlier on another issue; and his resignation had been widely interpreted as a signal for a more active policy. According to the account favoured by Mrs. Fischer, who, as a good German, has the habit of blaming German failures on the Russians, the " March action " was dictated from Moscow by Zinoviev and Bela Kun who, on the eve of the Kronstadt mutiny, were desperately

Studies in Revolution

anxious to score a German success to counter-balance troubles at home. Whatever the background of the attempt, its failure made a change of leadership inevitable. Paul Levi was succeeded as leader of the Right first by Ernst Meyer, another intellectual, and later by Heinrich Brandler, a worker from Saxony, who had all the caution of the old trade-union tradition; Mrs. Fischer together with her close associate Maslow soon emerged as the leaders of the Left.

The fiasco of the March rising in Germany discredited not only the German communist leaders, but Comintern itself and Zinoviev as its presiding genius. This resounding defeat for the cause of revolution in the country where, by every token, its prospects were most favourable, forced on Moscow a reconsideration of the whole time-table of world revolution; and it came at a time when Lenin had just announced the forced retreat on the home front embodied in NEP — the New Economic Policy of limited toleration and encouragement for private enterprise. It had become clear that Soviet Russia would have to go on living in a world of capitalist states for a much longer time than had at first been foreseen. The idea of marching straight forward to a world-wide victory of socialism had to be discarded. Strategic manœuvres, temporary retreats, political expedients of all kinds would be required to maintain and increase Soviet power until such time as the final goal was in sight. And this was just as true of foreign as of domestic policy. In international terms it meant that the star of Narkomindel

The Revolution that Failed

was in the ascendant, the star of Comintern on the wane. Chicherin began to eclipse Zinoviev.

This change raised an issue which has never ceased to be a source of embarrassment for the communist parties of the great countries other than Russia. Were these parties to pursue policies calculated to promote revolution at the earliest moment in their countries? Or were they, taking a broader view, to argue that the power of Soviet Russia, the one communist State, was the major asset of communism all over the world, and must therefore be maintained and supported even at the cost of temporary local sacrifices? This question took a particularly acute form in Germany, because Germany and Russia were linked by a common interest as the two great dissatisfied powers (though dissatisfied for different reasons) of the post-war settlement, the two pariah nations of European society. So long as Russia saw prospects of salvation in an imminent German revolution, the role of German communists was clear. But once the German revolution was not imminent and Soviet Russia had her back to the wall, the prudent course for Moscow might well be to stand shoulder to shoulder with the German Government against a world equally hostile to both. In this case the role of German communists must be, not to overthrow the German Government but to come to terms with it on the basis of a policy of friendship with the Soviet Government; and such a policy could perfectly well be defended, even from the standpoint of German communism.

Studies in Revolution

According to Ruth Fischer, whose testimony does not stand alone, this idea was first conceived by Radek when he was in prison in Berlin in the year 1919, and was then laughed out of court in Moscow. But after 1921, when NEP was in full swing and optimism about world revolution was no longer in fashion, things looked very different. In the next year the bargain was sealed by the famous Rapallo Treaty signed by Chicherin and Rathenau during the Genoa conference. It was about this time that the secret arrangements were started between the German Reichswehr and the Red Army for the purpose of evading the military provisions of the Versailles Treaty. In brief, the Reichswehr was to get facilities in Russia to carry out certain processes of manufacture and training, and the Red Army got in return technical training and equipment. But this new partnership between governments cast something of a blight on the German Communist Party. Radek, now chief agent of Comintern for Germany, cast the mantle of Moscow over Brandler, who wanted no rash revolutionary ventures and was prepared for temporary compromises with the Social-Democrats, and worked to oust Maslow and Ruth Fischer as the leaders of the Left. Naturally enough, Ruth Fischer has no love for Radek, and still less for Brandler, as every turn of her narrative shows. But the main facts here cannot be challenged. Radek was prepared to coquet even with the extreme German nationalists, just as they were prepared to coquet with Russia, on the ground of a common hatred of the western

The Revolution that Failed

allies. Many later patterns of policy can be traced in outline at this period.

At this point the destiny of the German Communist Party became involved not only in the changes of Soviet foreign policy, but in the feuds between Soviet leaders. By the late summer of 1923 the German workers were feeling the desperate pinch of the French occupation of the Ruhr and the German passive resistance policy; and the German Communist Party decided that the time was ripe for action. According to Mrs. Fischer, it was Stresemann's accession to power in August 1923 on a declared policy of coming to terms with the western Powers which caused a flurry of alarm in Moscow and prompted a decision by the Russian leaders that a German communist revolt against the Stresemann government was urgent. But this version, which fits in neatly with Mrs. Fischer's desire to lay every German failure at the door of Moscow, does not square with the facts. In Moscow the project of a German revolution was enthusiastically applauded only by Trotsky. Zinoviev, as usual, shilly-shallied; and Stalin preached caution. These divisions in Moscow meant that Russian assistance was half-hearted, and encouraged divisions and hesitations within the German party itself. Brandler, an excellent party organizer in ordinary times, was useless as a leader of armed insurrection. Elaborate preparations were going quietly forward when, in October, the Berlin Government struck first, sending the Reichswehr to depose the government of Saxony in which Brandler and two other

Studies in Revolution

communists had seats. This should have been the signal for a general rising. But the leaders were not ready; and, except for an unpremeditated outbreak at Hamburg which was suppressed with much bloodshed, nobody moved. The great project of a German communist revolution was snuffed out before it could start. " Seen from the inside ", writes Mrs. Fischer of this experience, " the communists were an insufficiently organized group of panic-stricken people, torn by factional quarrels, unable to come to a decision, and unclear about their own aims." That seems a not unfair epitaph on the largest Communist Party outside Russia.

The German defeat, like every other failure of a militant revolutionary policy, discredited Trotsky and Zinoviev and, by the same token, helped Stalin; and since it also meant the downfall of Brandler in Germany, Stalin paradoxically became, for the moment, the patron of the German Left. Manuilsky, who was a Stalin man, replaced Radek as principal Comintern agent in Germany. Mrs. Fischer passes rather lightly over the period when the Left communists in Germany hitched their waggon to Stalin's rising star. A relic of this period is a vivid and revealing description of Stalin in the summer of 1924, when he was just emerging into prominence among Bolshevist leaders:

At this Fifth World Congress Stalin became known to Comintern delegates for the first time. He glided silently, almost furtively, into the salons and corridors around St. Andrew's Hall. Smoking his pipe, wearing

The Revolution that Failed

the characteristic tunic and Wellington boots, he spoke softly and politely with small groups, assisted by an inconspicuous interpreter, presenting himself as the new type of Russian leader. The younger delegates were impressed by this pose as the revolutionary who despises revolutionary rhetoric, the down-to-earth organizer, whose quick decision and modernized methods would solve the problems in a changed world. The men around Zinoviev were old, fussy, out-moded.

Mrs. Fischer's narrative becomes a little confusing at this point; for, in her anxiety to exonerate her patron Zinoviev and herself of too-prolonged collaboration with the now hated Stalin, she has pushed back the split between Zinoviev and Stalin a good deal earlier than either evidence or probability allows.

At any rate, Zinoviev and Stalin were still on terms of friendship and co-operation, and Maslow and Mrs. Fischer, now the effective leaders of the KPD, were still in good standing at Moscow, when in April 1925 the Right in Germany decided to put forward Hindenburg as presidential candidate. The view of Comintern, supported by Maslow and Mrs. Fischer, was that the Communist candidate, Thälmann, should be withdrawn in order not to split the anti-Hindenburg vote. A majority of the KPD, inspired by Thälmann, decided otherwise, with the result that Hindenburg was elected. Neither of Mrs. Fischer's favourite generalizations — that the mistaken policies of the KPD were imposed on it from Moscow, and that she herself was a champion o the party against the domination of Moscow — held

Studies in Revolution

good on this occasion. It was only at the end of 1925 that Mrs. Fischer joined the Zinoviev opposition against Stalin. But by this time her popularity in the German party had been eclipsed by that of Thälmann, and in the following year Manuilsky had not much difficulty in bringing about her expulsion from the party as a Trotskyite. It is not a particularly edifying story. But it is not so simple, nor are the rights and wrongs so clear, as Mrs. Fischer's narrative might suggest to the uninitiated reader.

The party was now in a tragic decline, numerically, intellectually and as a political force. During the spurious prosperity of the Dawes period there could be no thought of a communist coup; and in the great depression which set in in 1929 the German Communist Party fell between two stools. It allowed the Nazis and the nationalists to make the pace in the campaign against the ineffective Weimar republic. On the other hand, the principle of non-co-operation with Social-Democrats, which had held ever since the debacle of 1923, prevented the communists from forming a common front against the Nazis. It is these years rather than the earlier period which justify one of the morals drawn by Mrs. Fischer: the difficulty which any Communist Party outside Russia has in standing up to the Russian party. A weak opposition party, often persecuted in its own country, is clearly no match for a party which has a victorious revolution behind it, and controls the affairs of a great nation. According to Mrs. Fischer, the influence of Moscow in the

196

The Revolution that Failed

German party was largely explicable by the number of jobs which Comintern with its large funds was able to offer to those who followed its line. This no doubt happened. But there is also the subtler influence of prestige, of rating in the scale of communist values. The weak, unsuccessful foreign party inevitably tends to take its cue from the strong successful Russian party; whenever a difference of view, or a difference of interest, manifests itself, the weaker yields to the stronger. Hence, it is only the exceptionally strong communist parties abroad which can hope to achieve some independence of Moscow. On a long view, it may well seem a disaster that the German communist movement after 1918 failed to develop its expected strength: had it done so, the one-sided identification of Russia and Communism which dominates world history to-day would have been avoided.

The failure of German communism is a phenomenon which deserves a more profound analysis than it has yet received, or than it receives from Mrs. Fischer, who is for the most part content to evoke the personal equation or the baneful influence of Comintern. Lenin, when he looked eagerly to the German revolution to save the revolution in Russia, believed — as Marxist doctrine entitled him to believe — that German communism was potentially a far more powerful, effective and earth-shaking force than Russian communism. Why did this not happen? One of the factors was obviously the unexpected strength of the nationalist come-back after the humiliation of Versailles. What seemed

Studies in Revolution

crushed had only been scotched. Moscow was not alone in the miscalculation of supposing that German national resentment could be encouraged up to a point, utilized and kept within safe bounds. Both Moscow and the western Powers from their different points of view overestimated the strength of German social-democracy. Both failed to take account of the absence in Germany of any of the conditions or traditions of western liberal democracy. The attempt to create a liberal democracy in Germany failed in 1848 and again after 1918; the attempt to create a social-democracy on the western pattern failed equally; and extreme Right and extreme Left confronted one another, just as they did in the Russia of 1917.

But in Germany, more than in any other country, the old pre-bourgeois ruling class, the feudal order of society with its military tradition, had succeeded in capturing and harnessing to its purposes the modern power of organized large-scale heavy industry. This was the achievement of Bismarck who, by his brilliant invention of the social services, also roped an influential section of the workers and the trade unions into a new power complex. This combination went into action in 1914; and, after the military disaster of 1918 and the political fiasco of the Weimar republic, it was still strong enough for Hitler to furbish it up once again in a rather more up-to-date and ostensibly popular guise. The strongest impression which the reading of Mrs. Fischer's book leaves on the mind is the terrifying power which the old forces in Germany continued

The Revolution that Failed

to exercise after 1918; and the chief reason of all for calling it a gloomy book is that it raises the question how far, in circumstances presenting so many analogies to the post-1918 period, these old forces are still alive and at work in Germany to-day.

13

STALIN: (1) THE ROAD TO POWER

IN the Soviet Union the name of Stalin has long been ranged with those of Marx, Engels and Lenin as an authoritative source, or at any rate an authoritative interpreter, of Bolshevik doctrine; and a collected edition of his works, now in course of publication in Moscow, was therefore overdue. It is being issued under the auspices of the Marx-Engels-Lenin Institute and will be complete in sixteen volumes, the last being devoted to his war-time speeches. The first volume covers the period 1901–1907, when Stalin — not yet generally known by this name — was an active revolutionary organizer in the Caucasus in the intervals of imprisonment and exile to Siberia. Most of the articles it contains were originally published in Georgian in fugitive underground periodicals and are now made accessible for the first time to the Russian reader. The editor explains that not all of Stalin's writings of this period have even now been re-discovered.

It has been customary among Stalin's enemies and detractors, beginning with Trotsky, to speak with contempt of his talents as a theorist. Compared with many of the others of his generation of Bolsheviks

200

Stalin: (1) *The Road to Power*

— not merely Lenin and Trotsky, but such men as Bukharin, Zinoviev and Radek — he has not been a fluent or prolific writer. No doubt the later volumes of this edition will be swelled by official pronouncements, the drafting of which may be attributed in part to his secretaries and advisers; it is even proposed to include the official Short History of the Russian Communist Party published in 1938 which, though prepared under Stalin's direction, certainly did not come from his pen. The pretension that Stalin ranks with Marx or Lenin as a thinker is exaggerated to the point of absurdity. Nevertheless the first volume of his works goes a long way to refute the legend fostered by Souvarine and others that the Soviet leader is a semi-literate ignoramus who repeats and distorts the already hackneyed ideas of others — a politician or a bureaucrat or an administrator unconcerned with theories and incapable of understanding them.

Nearly all the articles in this first volume are inspired by local controversies, mainly with the Mensheviks, who in Stalin's native Georgia always formed the more powerful wing of the party. The major items are an article of 1904 on the national question which foreshadows the famous article of 1912, both in its general conception and in its empirical conclusions, and invalidates the suggestion sometimes made that the later article was merely a transcription of Lenin's views; two articles on the party differences between Bolsheviks and Mensheviks; and a rather crude exposition of dialectical materialism in the form of a defence of Marxist

Studies in Revolution

socialism against anarchism. These writings reveal Stalin, not indeed as an original thinker, but as an active and competent propagandist and popularizer and as a faithful disciple of the Bolshevik creed. Lenin is mentioned by name only a few times (Stalin's first meeting with him occurred at the end of 1905, but is not referred to here); and, on the only two noteworthy occasions during this period in which Lenin's personal opinion was rejected and overruled by the majority of the party, Stalin supported the majority. He wrote in favour of boycotting the elections to the first Duma, where Lenin was for participation; and he voted at the fourth party congress in 1906 for the distribution of land to the peasants, where Lenin was for nationalization.

It is, however, apparent that even at this early period Stalin was, consciously or unconsciously, moulded by Lenin and by a particular aspect of Lenin. The acute and bitter controversies which marked the formative years of the party all turned in one way or another on an issue which involved both ideas and organization. Was the workers' movement to be supplied with its philosophy, its leadership and its initiative by a small and highly organized group of determined revolutionaries, who must, in the nature of things, be drawn mainly from the intellectuals? Or was the party to regard itself as the servant and follower of the workers and rely for its initiative on the " spontaneous " urge to revolution which intolerable conditions would sooner or later breed among them? Lenin, the passionate

Stalin: (1) *The Road to Power*

protagonist of the first view, contemptuously dubbed the supporters of the alternative view " tail-enders ", and amid many backslidings built up the Bolshevik party almost single-handed on his own narrow but powerful conception of the way in which revolutions are made.

Stalin emerged from the ruck as one of those who stood without hesitation for Lenin's policy. It was not for nothing that Lenin in a much-quoted letter referred to him as the " wonderful Georgian " and made him, in 1912, a member of the central committee of the party. From the first, Stalin accepted, perhaps with even less reservation than Lenin himself, the obligation of the party to lead, to organize and to fight. " Our party", he says in one of these early articles, " is not a collection of individual chatterers, but an organization of leaders." And again : " Only *unity* of opinion can unite the members of the party into one centralized party. If unity of opinion collapses, the party collapses." Lenin's pamphlet *What is to be Done?* which expresses these ideas in their clearest and most forcible form becomes his bible, and the writings of his early period bristle with praise of organization and scorn for those who depend on the efficacy of " spontaneous " forces within the working class. " The spontaneous workers' movement ", he quotes from Lenin, " so long as it remains spontaneous, so long as it is not united with socialist consciousness, submits itself to bourgeois ideology and is inevitably drawn to such submission." The formula is a " union of the workers' movement with socialism " ;

Studies in Revolution

and this can be achieved only by a small organized party of high intellectual as well as moral quality, imbued with complete mastery of the intricacies of revolutionary socialist doctrine.

The danger plainly inherent in this doctrine is the temptation to exalt organization as a necessary means to revolution, and revolution as an end in itself. Formally speaking, the Bolshevik theorists — Stalin perhaps less than Lenin — guard themselves against this danger. One passage in these early writings oddly recalls the optimistic conviction of pious Victorians that the good, by some ultimate law of progress, will prevail over the bad.

If the teaching of the anarchists represents the truth, it will, of course, necessarily make its own way and gather the masses round it. If it is unsubstantial and built on a false foundation, then it will not hold for long and will vanish into the air.

This optimism is supported elsewhere by a reference to the famous Hegelian doctrine — in view of the recent attitude of the Russian philosophical schools to German philosophy in general and Hegel in particular, it is interesting to find Stalin defending Hegel — of the identity of the real and the rational. Marxism will triumph, says Stalin explicitly, because it is rational: what is irrational is doomed to perish. Yet the first critics of Hegel perceived clearly the dilemma of finding any criterion of what is rational other than what, in fact, succeeds; and the youthful Stalin is no more successful than they in resolving it. The cause of revolution is the rational, and therefore the good,

Stalin: (1) *The Road to Power*

cause, because its inevitability can be scientifically proved. But the validity of the proof can only be tested by the event; and if your calculations should turn out to be wrong, it would mean, not that the science was false but that your application of it was faulty. The door is thus thrown wide open for sheer empiricism.

Beyond doubt some distinction, at any rate of emphasis, can be drawn between the empiricism of Lenin and the empiricism of Stalin. " Proletarian socialism ", writes Stalin at this time, " is built not on sentimental feelings, not on abstract ' justice ', not on love for the proletariat, but on scientific principles." Stalin in his maturity might have expressed himself more cautiously. Yet the impression remains that Lenin's dryness concealed a certain degree of humanity, perhaps of sincere " love for the proletariat ", which was absent from the make-up of his more ruthless disciple. Lenin's earlier writings are marked by a strong tinge of Utopianism, which was shed slowly and reluctantly when he was brought into contact with the stern realities and responsibilities entailed by the exercise of power. In *State and Revolution*, written on the eve of October 1917, Lenin strongly denounced those who regarded the State as anything but a necessary evil or sought to obscure the Marxist doctrine of the dying away of the State as a condition of the communist order. Even when this dream had to be relegated to the comparatively remote future, Lenin continued to insist on the need for " direct democracy ", for self-government from below, for the

Studies in Revolution

ordinary citizen himself learning to administer and control, as the antidote to State bureaucracy. Of such visions, unsubstantial as they proved to be, there is little or no trace in Stalin's speeches or writings.

Such differences of doctrine and emphasis as may be detected between Lenin and Stalin can, however, be plausibly attributed not so much to personal divergences of outlook or temperament as to differences in the historical situation which confronted them. Lenin, for all his insistence on the leadership of a highly trained and organized group of professional revolutionaries, knew that revolutions are made by the masses and that to win the active, or even the passive, support of the masses something more than organization and leadership was required. He knew that even discontent with existing conditions, indispensable though that was as a starting-point, was not enough to sustain a revolutionary ardour. The vision of a new world — in which men, freed from the oppression of bourgeois capitalism and of the bourgeois State, would learn to govern themselves and to organize the processes of production and distribution for the common good — was necessary to fire the revolutionary imagination. Lenin inherited the splendid vision from a long line of nineteenth-century socialists. He accepted it, sincerely believed in it, and justified his policies by the prospect of its realization. If, after the first few months of power, the prospect seemed to recede into a remote future and the difficulties of its realization became increasingly apparent, there is no

206

Stalin: (1) *The Road to Power*

evidence that Lenin ever abandoned his faith in it.

Stalin's career was different. Lenin appraised his merits as a professional revolutionary. His function was to organize; and in this he was supreme. He never sought to kindle the enthusiasm of the masses; for he lacked altogether the temperament, and perhaps the convictions, necessary for such an achievement. His stepping-stone to power was an appointment that required exactly those gifts of organization which he possessed — the secretary-ship of the party; and he rose to power because, after 1922, it was no longer revolutionary enthusiasm but capacity to organize which the historical situation demanded. In this sense Stalin was a product of the revolution in its later phase. He inherited it from its chief progenitor, and for more than twenty years he directed and tamed and moulded it. To inquire how far he shaped its course by his personal intervention and initiative, and how far he was the agent of inevitable forces working themselves out to a predestined end, is merely to raise the eternal question of the position of the great man in history.

One of the most marked features which distinguishes Stalin's outlook from Lenin's and gives Stalin a crucial place in revolutionary history is the shift from the international to the national standpoint. Here, too, differences of background played their part. Lenin spent the most formative years of his life abroad, and spoke the principal European languages; and his revolutionary doctrine was international to the core. Stalin knows no language but Russian and Georgian and has never left Russia

Studies in Revolution

except for visits to three or four party conferences before 1914 and for his recent excursions to Teheran and Potsdam. His Georgian origin accounted for his early special studies of nationalism and for his choice as People's Commissar for Nationalities in 1917; but it does not seem to have had any important influence on him — unless it was to give an almost fanatical intensity to his Soviet patriotism. It was thus no accident that made him the sponsor of " socialism in one country " in the 1920s, the antagonist of the internationally minded Trotsky, and the protagonist of the revival of Russian national sentiment, after its revolutionary eclipse, in the 1930s. When war came in 1941 he was already the national rather than the revolutionary hero. His relations with the army seem from the outset to have been easy. He had done much, even before the war, to restore its prestige and to bring it back to its former place of honour in the national life. The war brought his finest qualities and capacities to their full fruition; and his designation as Marshal of the Soviet Union in March 1943 could be regarded as a natural culmination of his career rather than as a mere concession to the exigencies of war.

It is no doubt a paradox that one who appeared on the scene as a revolutionary conspirator should be acclaimed to-day principally for his patriotic devotion to his country and for his unflinching leadership in time of war. The frontispiece to his collected works significantly shows him in his marshal's uniform. But such paradoxes are not without precedent in the history of revolutions; and Lenin,

Stalin: (1) *The Road to Power*

though his revolutionary convictions were far more deep-rooted than Stalin's, might well have undergone some such transformation, had he lived long enough. The criticisms which will have to be taken into account in the ultimate assessment of Stalin's record relate not so much to the ends which he pursued and achieved as to the means by which he pursued and achieved them. Lenin, in his so-called testament, described Stalin as " too rough " and referred to him as deficient in " loyalty ". His rise to power was beyond doubt marked by an unusual skill in the less amiable arts of political intrigue. He worked beneath the surface, undermined established reputations, held back while others committed themselves to untenable positions and then struck, and struck hard. He was a cunning, vindictive and ruthless antagonist; and the indignities and brutalities which he heaped on his fallen adversaries while they had many precedents in the Russian tradition, were shocking to western minds.

Yet, if Stalin introduced or reintroduced into Russian history a narrow and systematically ruthless intolerance which the first enthusiasm of the revolution seemed to have expelled or mitigated, this was in the character of the time as much as of the man. The Bolshevik revolution, like other revolutions, began in an atmosphere of idealism which bordered on Utopia. But soon opposition from within and from without provoked repression, and violence bred violence. Terror was soon being applied not only against survivors of the *ancien régime* and of the bourgeoisie but against other revolutionary parties

Studies in Revolution

which attempted to maintain an independent existence. Even Lenin's prestige and his genius for persuasion did not suffice in his later years to maintain party unity without threats of expulsion and limitations on the freedom of speech and opinion of its members. When Lenin disappeared from the scene, profound rifts quickly revealed themselves, and the weapons of repression hitherto used only against dissentients outside the party were, logically and almost inevitably, turned against dissentients within it.

The judgment of history on Stalin's role will depend in part on the wider judgment which it passes on the Bolshevik revolution. The claim of that revolution to have inaugurated a " new civilization " has been asserted and contested. But, on any view, it was one of the great turning-points in history, comparable with the French revolution and perhaps surpassing it in significance. No country in the world has remained indifferent to it, no form of government has been able to evade its challenge, no political or economic theory has escaped its searching criticism; nor, according to all signs and portents, has its influence yet reached a peak. The collected edition of Stalin's writings and speeches, while it will probably add little that is specific to existing knowledge of the man or his work, will help to place it in perspective, and will constitute a historical document of the first importance.

14

STALIN: (2) THE DIALECTICS
OF STALINISM

EVERY biography of Stalin is necessarily a "political biography"; for Stalin is a politician to his finger-tips, and there is no other capacity in which either contemporaries or posterity are likely to interest themselves in him. What Mr. Deutscher means by giving his new biography of Stalin [1] this sub-title is, perhaps, not so much that he has wasted less time than the hagiographers of Moscow or than hostile biographers like Souvarine and Trotsky on more or less mythical episodes, creditable or discreditable, of Stalin's youth and personal life, but rather that he intends his book as an analysis of his hero's political achievement. This is, in fact, what it is; and the intention has been brilliantly executed. The usual difficulty of political biography, the difficulty of separating the record of the man from the history of his time, scarcely arises in dealing with Stalin. Since Lenin's death Stalin's career and the history of Soviet Russia have been inseparable. Nothing that belongs to the one can be regarded as

[1] I. Deutscher, *Stalin*. A Political Biography. Oxford University Press. London: Cumberlege. 25s.

Studies in Revolution

irrelevant to the other. A story so dramatic as Stalin's cannot be dull. Mr. Deutscher has missed none of the points and has written a book which, among its other merits, is absorbing to read. But it is absorbing in part because, in all the excitement of the external detail, he has never lost sight of his central theme of the nature of Stalin's achievement and his place in the history of the revolution.

It need hardly be said that this, like everything else about Stalin, is highly controversial. It raises many questions which, like most of the profound questions of history, cannot be readily answered with a simple yes or no. Is Stalin the disciple of Marx or an Oriental despot? Has he fulfilled or renounced the heritage of Lenin? Has he built " socialism in one country " or blighted the prospects of socialism throughout the world for a generation to come? Has he — a second Peter the Great — Europeanized Russia, or — a second Genghis Khan — made Russia part of a vast Asiatic empire? Is he a nationalist assiduously seeking to increase the prestige and power of Russia, or an internationalist concerned to bring about the universal triumph of a revolutionary creed? These questions are susceptible of many different answers. Mr. Deutscher's book will enable the reader, if not to answer them, at any rate to ask them with greater understanding.

History never stands still — least of all in the middle of a revolution. What Lenin created and what Stalin inherited from him was a constantly changing entity, not a static system, but a process

Stalin: (2) *The Dialectics of Stalinism*

of development. It was a process in which, to borrow the Hegelian idiom, thesis was continually begetting antithesis, so that the question whether Stalin continued or negated the work of Lenin may reflect a distinction of language rather than of substance. Put less abstractly, the truth seems to be that every revolution is succeeded by its own reaction and that, when Lenin was withdrawn from the scene, the Russian revolution had already entered this secondary stage of its course. The once current slogan, "Stalin is the Lenin of to-day", did not assert that Stalin was the Lenin of 1917, but that he was performing the function which Lenin himself would have had to perform if he had remained the leader of the revolution ten years later. Even so, it was not wholly true. But it contained some elements of the truth.

The early Bolsheviks were students of history and knew what happens to revolutions: they feared that their revolution, too, would meet its Thermidor. But the spell of Bonaparte made them assume that the source of danger was a dictator in shining armour. It was this assumption which proved fatal to Trotsky and smoothed Stalin's path to power. In Mr. Deutscher's words:

It had always been admitted that history might repeat itself, and that a directory or a single usurper might once again climb to power on the back of the revolution. It was taken for granted that the Russian usurper would, like his French prototype, have a personality possessed of brilliance and legendary fame won in battles. The mask of Bonaparte seemed to fit Trotsky only too well.

Studies in Revolution

Indeed, it might have fitted any personality with the exception of Stalin. In this lay part of his strength.

Thus it was that Stalin became, if not " the Lenin of to-day ", the Bonaparte of to-day, the heir of Lenin as Bonaparte was the heir of Robespierre, the man who chained and disciplined the revolution, and consolidated its achievements, and garbled its doctrines, and wedded it to a great national power, and spread its influence throughout the world.

Yet this, too, was not the whole truth. For, while history sometimes repeats itself in unexpected disguises, every historical situation is none the less unique. The odd thing is that Stalin, unpredictably and seemingly in spite of himself, became, unlike Bonaparte, a revolutionary in his own right. More than ten years after Lenin's revolution, Stalin made a second revolution without which Lenin's revolution would have run out into the sand. In this sense Stalin continued and fulfilled Leninism, though the slogan of " socialism in one country ", under which he made his revolution, was the rejection of what. Lenin believed (the efforts of Stalin's theorists to father it on Lenin were childishly disingenuous) and Lenin would have recoiled in horror from some of the methods by which the second revolution was made.

Intellectually, as Mr. Deutscher is careful to point out, " socialism in one country " made no new and original contribution to doctrine. It was not even very coherent, since Stalin himself, clinging firmly to the ill-fitting garments of Marxist orthodoxy, admitted that socialism could never be com-

Stalin: (2) *The Dialectics of Stalinism*

pletely and securely realized in one country isolated in a capitalist world. But psychologically and politically it was a brilliant discovery; and it does not seriously detract from Stalin's political genius to say that, like other great discoveries, its author stumbled on it unawares. It happened in 1924, the year in which Lenin died, at the height of the controversy with Trotsky and between two editions of Stalin's *Foundations of Leninism*. The first edition contained a passage which read too much like an endorsement of Trotsky's " permanent revolution ". In the second edition this gave place to a clear and unequivocal statement that socialism could be built in one country — even in backward, peasant Russia.

When Lenin died, orthodox Bolshevism had run into a blind alley. All agreed that the first task in 1917 had been to complete the unfinished bourgeois revolution in Russia; and this, it could fairly be said, had been done. All Bolsheviks agreed (as against the Mensheviks) that, in completing the bourgeois revolution, they would pass over directly into the stage of the socialist revolution; this, too, had happened. But at this point all Bolsheviks, from Lenin downwards, had confidently assumed that the torch kindled in Russia would ignite the socialist revolution in western Europe, and that the European proletariat would take up the burden of completing the socialist revolution and building a socialist society. This task — Lenin had said it again and again — was too heavy for backward Russia to carry out alone.

Studies in Revolution

Unfortunately this time-table had not been realized. Revolution in Europe, which seemed certain in 1919 and imminent in 1920 when the Red Army was outside Warsaw, still unaccountably tarried. In the autumn of 1923, when the German proletariat for the third or fourth time since 1918 suffered a crushing defeat (recriminations about who was to blame did not help), it came to be gradually understood in Moscow that the European revolution was still a long way off. But what, on this new hypothesis, was the role of the Russian Bolsheviks? Nobody denied, it was true, that one of their tasks was to proceed with the building of socialism in Russia: Trotsky was pressing the case for intensive planning and industrialization long before it had been taken up by Stalin. But, none the less, since it seemed to follow from the orthodox doctrine that it was not possible to get very far in Russia in the absence of revolution elsewhere, a sense of unreality and frustration could hardly be avoided. The rank and file, if not the party *intelligentsia*, needed the stimulus and inspiration of a finite goal set in a not too remote future, and dependent for its realization, not on incalculable events in far-away Europe but on their own efforts.

This need was brilliantly met by "socialism in one country". Mr. Deutscher's imaginative reconstruction of what the new slogan meant to Stalin's followers cannot be bettered:

Of course we are looking forward to international revolution. Of course we have been brought up in the school of Marxism; and we know that contemporary

Stalin: (2) *The Dialectics of Stalinism*

social and political struggles are, by their very nature, international. Of course we still believe the victory of the proletariat in the west to be near; and we are bound in honour to do what we can to speed it up. But — and this was a very big, a highly suggestive " but " — do not worry so much about all that international revolution. Even if it were to be delayed indefinitely, even if it were never to occur, we in this country are capable of developing into a fully fledged classless society. Let us then concentrate on our great constructive task.

An English empiricist might have said: " Let the theory take care of itself, and get on with the job ". Stalin the Marxist had to wrap it up in a tiresome paraphernalia of doctrine. But it came to much the same thing.

On the slogan of " socialism in one country " Stalin rode to power — to become the prisoner of the spirits he had conjured up. For there was, it turned out, something to be said for the older, more cautious, less empirical Marxism of an earlier generation, however inconvenient its application might be to the Russia of the later nineteen-twenties. The hard core of reality behind the division of Europe into east and west was the frontier running approximately from Danzig to Trieste, the frontier between developed capitalist Europe, where the proletariat was already a force, and undeveloped peasant Europe, where the hold of feudalism had hardly yet been broken. Perhaps, after all, Lenin and Trotsky — and Stalin himself down to the autumn of 1924 — had been right when they argued that the victory of socialism could not be achieved

Studies in Revolution

in backward Russia without a socialist revolution in the proletarian countries of western Europe. Perhaps even — though nobody dared to hint this in Russia — the Mensheviks had not been altogether wrong when they maintained that it was not possible to pass over direct from the bourgeois to the socialist stage of the revolution and that socialism could be built only on an established foundation of bourgeois capitalism.

Naturally the answer to these questions turned partly on what was meant by socialism. Stalin had undertaken to produce " socialism in one country ". Whatever he produced must clearly be called " socialism "; moreover, the Five-year Plan and the collectivization of agriculture were unimpeachable items in a revolutionary socialist programme. Nevertheless it would be a mistake to assume that these measures were imposed on Stalin, or imposed by Stalin on Russia, on the strength of any slogan or programme, whether " socialism in one country " or another. They were imposed by the objective situation which Soviet Russia in the later nineteen-twenties had to face.

The Leninist revolution had by this time run its course. The key industries had been nationalized and, in a superficial and fragmentary way, " planned ", but not fitted into an economy designed as a single unit. The land had been given to the peasants. Every device had been tried to step up agricultural production — the key to the whole structure. The *kulak* had been first terrorized for the benefit of the poor peasant, then encouraged

218

Stalin: (2) *The Dialectics of Stalinism*

to fend for himself under NEP; Bukharin had even told him that he was fulfilling the highest purposes of socialism by enriching himself. But none of these devices had more than a momentary success. Since any substantial assistance from the capitalist countries had to be ruled out, the economy could not advance on socialist lines, or on any other lines, without an increased yield from agriculture; and this was conceivable only through the restoration of large-scale farming and the introduction of mechanization. Short of a relapse into conditions more primitive than those destroyed by the revolution, or of an unconditional surrender to foreign capitalism — and neither was a conceivable solution — there was no road open save the hard road which Russia was to travel under Stalin's leadership and the banner of " socialism in one country ".

The most baffling feature of Stalin's career is that he carried out a revolution which was no less far-reaching than the revolution of 1917, and was in many senses its logical and necessary completion, at a time when the popular tide of revolutionary enthusiasm had ebbed away, and to the accompaniment of many " Thermidorean " symptoms of counter-revolution. It was thus that Trotsky could find ground for denouncing Stalin as a counter-revolutionary and as the destroyer of the revolution. Mr. Deutscher sums up the difference between the Leninist and Stalinist revolutions by calling the first a revolution " from below " and the second a revolution " from above ". The distinction must not be pressed too far. Lenin specifically rejected

Studies in Revolution

the idea that revolutions are made by the spontaneous enthusiasm of the masses; he believed in, and imposed, strict revolutionary discipline. Stalin, whose theory on this point did not differ from Lenin's, could not have executed his colossal task unless he had been able to rely on a broad base of popular support. Yet it is clear that Stalin had to contend with far more apathy and disillusionment in the masses, far more opposition and intrigue in the party *élite*, than Lenin had ever known, and was driven to apply correspondingly harsher and more ruthless measures of discipline. It is also significant that most of the appeals by which Stalin justified his revolution were to instincts normally the reverse of revolutionary — to law and order, to the sanctity of the family, to the defence of the fatherland and to the virtue of cultivating one's own garden: it was as a restless international adventurer, a man who cared nothing for his country, a champion of " permanent revolution ", that Trotsky was pilloried.

Stalin thus presents two faces to the world — a revolutionary-Marxist face and a national-Russian face — two aspects which are partly conflicting and partly complementary. And if the gradation from the Leninist to the Stalinist revolution is expressed in these terms, it may perhaps be said that the one was essentially designed as an international revolution occurring in Russia and to that extent adapting itself to Russian conditions, and the other as a national revolution which no doubt carried with it its international demands and its international

Stalin: (2) *The Dialectics of Stalinism*

implications, but was primarily concerned with establishing itself. Mr. Deutscher quotes somewhere the retort of Dostoevsky's Grand Inquisitor to Christ: " We have corrected Thy deed ". One of the ways in which Stalin corrected Lenin's deed was to root it firmly and tenaciously in the national soil. This was, after all, the central tenet of Stalin's philosophy. He believed, what Lenin doubted or denied, that socialism could be built in an isolated Russian State.

The marriage of the international ideals of the revolution to national sentiment was bound to occur. It had happened in the French revolution. It had begun to happen in Soviet Russia long before Stalin took charge of her destinies: the first occasion on which patriotic and revolutionary feelings were conspicuously blended and intertwined was the war against Poland in 1920. The long isolation of Soviet Russia, the persistent hostility of the greater part of the capitalist world were bound to reinforce the trend. When Stalin in 1924 proclaimed the possibility of " socialism in one country " he was, without knowing it, appealing to the deep springs of a national pride which for ten years had been not only dead but damned. He told his followers that Russians could do precisely what Lenin and all other Bolsheviks had hitherto believed them incapable of doing. " Russia will do it for herself ", he might have said, parodying Cavour. The five-year plans were launched under the slogans of " catching up " and " overtaking " the capitalist countries, of beating them at their own game.

Studies in Revolution

It was thus that Stalin became the reviver of Russian patriotism, the first leader explicitly to reverse the international or anti-national attitude which had dominated the early stages of the revolution. The first Bolshevik historians had depicted previous Russian history in the main as a long series of barbarities and scandals. " Backward " was the standard epithet to attach to the name " Russia ". Stalin changed all that. He put out of business altogether the " Marxist " school of historians headed by Pokrovsky (whom Lenin had highly praised and valued), and rehabilitated the Russian past. A new drive was required in place of the cooling revolutionary ardour in order to render tolerable the hardships of industrialization and to steel resistance to potential enemies. Stalin found it in nationalism. New-found enthusiasms tend to exaggeration; and victory over Hitler was an intoxicating achievement. Soviet nationalism since the war has taken some forms which western observers have thought sinister and others which they have thought absurd. But it has, perhaps, not differed as much as is sometimes supposed from that of other great Powers at the moment of their ascent to greatness.

Other aspects of Stalin's return to a national tradition may weigh more heavily against him in the scales of history. The real charge against Stalinism is that it abandoned those fruitful elements of the western tradition which were embodied in the original Marxism, and substituted for them retrograde and oppressive elements drawn from the Russian tradition. Marxism stood on the shoulders

Stalin: (2) *The Dialectics of Stalinism*

of western bourgeois liberal democracy, and, while ultimately rejecting it, assumed and adopted many of its achievements. This is the meaning of the insistence in the *Communist Manifesto* that bourgeois democracy had been in its day a progressive liberating force and that the proletarian revolution could come only as a second step after the consummation of the bourgeois revolution; and many of the first legislative acts and declarations of the Soviet regime in Russia were inspired as much by the ideals of bourgeois democracy as by those of socialism. When the moment came to pass on to the realization of socialism, this meant, not that democratic ideals would be abandoned, but that they would be fulfilled, as the degenerate bourgeois democracies of the west were no longer capable of fulfilling them.

Such was Lenin's dream in 1917. But it was from the Marxist standpoint an anomaly, and from the standpoint of socialism a tragedy, that the first victorious socialist revolution should have occurred in what was economically, socially and politically the most backward of the great countries of Europe. The workers who were called on to build the first socialist order had been for generations the victims of economic poverty, social inequality and political repression more extreme than those prevailing in any other great country. The socialist order in Russia could draw neither on the wealth created by past capitalist enterprise nor on the political experience fostered by bourgeois democracy. At the very end of his life Lenin began to realize to the full the handicaps imposed by these shortcomings. A

Studies in Revolution

passage quoted by Mr. Deutscher from his speech at the last party congress he attended penetrates to the taproots of " Stalinism " :

If the conquering nation is more cultured than the vanquished nation, the former imposes its culture on the latter; but if the opposite is the case, the vanquished nation imposes its culture on the conqueror.

Something of the same sort, Lenin continued, could happen between classes. In the RSFSR the culture of the vanquished classes, " miserable and low as it is, is higher than that of our responsible Communist administrators " ; the old Russian bureaucracy, in virtue of this relatively higher level of culture, was vanquishing the victorious, but ignorant and inexperienced, Communists.

This was the danger which Lenin, with the clear-sightedness of genius, diagnosed in what he saw around him in the fifth year of the revolution. It was implicit in the continued isolation of socialist Russia from the rest of the world and in the necessity of building " socialism in one country ". International Marxism and international socialism, planted in Russian soil and left to themselves, found their international character exposed to the constant sapping and mining of the Russian national tradition which they had supposedly vanquished in 1917. Ten years later, when Lenin was dead, the leaders who had most conspicuously represented the international and western elements in Bolshevism, — Trotsky, Zinoviev and Kamenev, not to mention minor figures like Radek, Krasin and Rakovsky — had all disappeared; the mild and pliable Bukharin

Stalin: (2) *The Dialectics of Stalinism*

was soon to follow. The hidden forces of the Russian past — autocracy, bureaucracy, political and cultural conformity — took their revenge, not by destroying the revolution but by harnessing it to themselves in order to fulfil it in a narrow national framework. These forces carried Stalin to power and made him what he remains to-day, the enigmatic protagonist both of international revolution and of national tradition.

The reader of Stalin's biography, holding this thread in his hand, will be able to pick his way through a maze whose intricacies appear at first sight infinite, but whose general pattern gradually reveals itself. It is not perhaps an issue which lends itself profitably to discussion in terms of praise and blame. The isolation of the Russian revolution compelled it to rely on its own resources; in turning its back on the outside world it increased its own isolation. Each step drove Russia farther back into her past. When Stalin determined to drive the revolution to its logical conclusion at all costs through industrialization and collectivization, the least fanciful observers were reminded of Peter the Great. When he resolved to protect himself against the potential dangers of treachery in the event of foreign attack by eliminating every possible rival, men thought of Ivan the Terrible. Party orthodoxy came to play the same constricting role as ecclesiastical orthodoxy had played in medieval Russia, with its claim to a monopoly over all philosophy and literature and art. Yet it would be unfair to suppose that Stalin deliberately and consciously sought isolation. Again

Studies in Revolution

and again gestures of approach were made to the western world. But only under the stress of war could the barriers be overcome. Once it was over, the iron curtain again descended. The rift between the Russian revolution and the west was too wide to be bridged.

At the end of 1949 Stalin celebrated his seventieth birthday. He has led his country victoriously through its greatest war and surmounted the immediate difficulties of demobilization and reconstruction as smoothly as any of the belligerents. To all outward seeming he stands at the pinnacle of his own and his nation's power. In spite of the familiar injunction to call no man happy till he is dead, the temptation is strong to assume that the shape of Stalin's career is fixed and will not be substantially modified by anything yet to come. Even, however, if this assumption is correct, it does not mean that Stalin's place in history is already fixed — or will be for a generation to come. We can still only begin to see, " through a glass, darkly ", what has been happening in the last thirty years. We dimly perceive that the revolution of 1917, itself the product of the upheaval of 1914, was a turning-point in world history certainly comparable in magnitude with the French revolution a century and a quarter earlier, and perhaps surpassing it. The significance of Lenin's work is just coming into focus.

But of Stalin it is still too early to speak ; Stalin's work is still too plainly subject to the distorting lens of excessive propinquity. How far has he generalized the experience of the revolution of 1917 and how

Stalin: (2) The Dialectics of Stalinism

far particularized it? Has he carried it forward to its triumphant conclusion, or destroyed it altogether, or twisted it out of shape? The answer — and one which to some extent begs the question — can for the present be given only in terms of the concluding sentences of Mr. Deutscher's biography:

> The better part of Stalin's work is as certain to outlast Stalin himself as the better parts of the works of Cromwell and Napoleon have outlasted them. But in order to save it for the future and to give it its full value, history may yet have to cleanse and reshape Stalin's work as sternly as it once cleansed and reshaped the work of the English revolution after Cromwell and of the French after Napoleon.

THE END